Introducing SSADM4+

The SSADM Management Board

SSADM was first developed by the CCTA, the Government Centre for Information Systems, in the early 1980s. SSADM has been continually improved since then by the CCTA and has become the most widely used analysis and design method in the UK and increasingly in Europe and beyond.

SSADM remains a public domain method and is protected by Crown copyright. The on-going development, management and marketing of SSADM is now the responsibility of a newly formed partnership between three organizations: CCTA, NCC Blackwell, and the International SSADM Users Group. A senior management board comprising representatives of each of these three organizations has the prime responsibility of ensuring that the investment made by the users in SSADM is protected as the method moves forward. The SSADM Management Board was formed in 1995 alongside the launch of the new version of the method, SSADM4+ version 4.2, and the System Development Library.

The SSADM Management Board has produced a White Paper setting out the key areas for future development of SSADM4+ and the System Development Library. The next update to SSADM4+ will include the addition of further guidance on graphical user interface design in the SSADM manuals. Future developments are likely to include the further integration of business analysis and work practice into the method, better coverage of small systems, further moves towards supporting object-orientation, support for re-engineering and legacy systems projects, and extending the guidance on customizing and applying SSADM to different project situations.

For more information on the method and the SSADM Management Board please contact:
Anne Kitson, NCC Blackwell, 108 Cowley Road, Oxford OX4 1JF, telephone: 01865 791100, fax: 01865 798219, email: akitson@blackwellpublishers.co.uk.

For further information regarding CCTA products please contact:
CCTA Library, Rosebery Court, St Andrews Business Park, Norwich NR7 0HS, telephone: 01603 704930

Acknowledgements: John Hall of Model Systems Ltd and Caroline Slater of Cray Systems AIMS, under contract to CCTA, are acknowledged for the development of the original text and diagrams for SSADM4+ version 4.2.

Siemens Nixdorf Informationssysteme AG and Model Systems, under contract to CCTA, are acknowledged for contributions to the original EU-rent case study which was first published in the ISE library volume 'Distributed Systems: Application Development'. The EU-rent case study has been further developed by Model Systems, and is used throughout these manuals.

System Development Library

Introducing SSADM4+

BLACKWELL *Publishers*

The text of this introduction was written by Colin Bentley.

© Crown Copyright, 1996
First published 1996
2 4 6 8 10 9 7 5 3 1

Published by agreement with the Controller of Her Majesty's Stationery Office by
NCC Blackwell Ltd
108 Cowley Road
Oxford OX4 1JF
UK

Blackwell Publishers Inc
238 Main Street
Cambridge,
Massachusetts 02142
USA

British Library Cataloguing in Publication Data
A CIP catalogue record for this book is available from the
British Library.

Library of Congress Cataloging-in-Publication Data
Bentley, Colin.
    Introducing SSADM4+ : version 4.2 / Colin Bentley.
      p.   cm. – (Systems development library)
    Includes index.
    ISBN 1-85554-766-X (alk. paper)
    1. System design. 2. Electronic data processing–Structured techniques. I. Title. II. Series.
    QA76.9.S88B46   1996
    005.1'2–dc20   95-52335
                                                          CIP

ISBN 185554 766X

Typeset in 10 on 12 pt Times by Archetype
Printed in Great Britain by T. J. Press Ltd., Padstow, Cornwall
This book is printed on acid-free paper

Contents

Preface

Three concerns continue to dominate information system development – delivering business solutions, delivering them quickly and getting return on investment on legacy systems. These concerns have to be addressed in an environment of rapidly developing technology, a changing role for central Information Technology in organizations and a move from individual to group Information System support.

An increasingly important issue is the need for IS architectures within which application systems can be developed.

Information systems need to become integral parts of business systems. A significant problem is the failure of many business process modelling approaches to separate the essential business process from organizational structure and work practice. SSADM4+ has enhancements which overcome this problem.

SSADM4+ is part of the System Development Library which includes a wide range of publications supporting the use of SSADM, and other related methods such as COMPACT for analysis and design of office technology systems.

Rapid Application Development approaches can be easily adopted with SSADM4+. RAD can be significantly enhanced by applying SSADM's 3-schema Specification Architecture as the basis for development.

SSADM has come a long way since its inception and it looks well-placed to improve its standing as the most popular and useful analysis and design method for business information systems. This book describes SSADM4+ and discusses the future of the on-going development of the method.

Part I

INTRODUCTION

1

Introduction

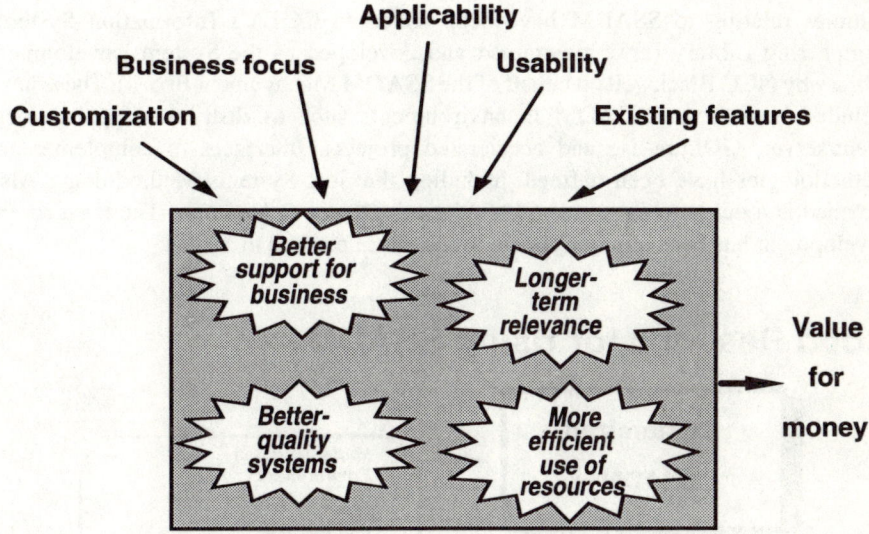

Figure 1.1 Business Benefits of SSADM4+

It is common knowledge how important information systems are in business, and also how high the risks associated with their development can be, e.g. cost overruns, late delivery, dissatisfied customers. The challenge for management is to minimize the risk of building systems which won't meet the needs of the business. Analysis and design methods help by investigating in a thorough and systematic way what the new system needs to do and what the best options are likely to be. Experience shows that without such investigation in the early stages of a project, its chances of success are greatly reduced.

SSADM is a powerful analysis and design method. It uses a range of techniques to specify business system requirements and to design an appropriate IT solution. SSADM has been around for almost fifteen years and is still improving. It is recognized as the key analysis and design method by the National Computing Centre and British Computer Society, who base the IS Examination Board's examination for computer

3

analysts and designers on it. More than 5,000 people have now passed the ISEB examination for SSADM certification and over 120 companies have signed the SSADM Trade Mark agreements to provide services, ensuring that there is widespread and comprehensive support for SSADM users.

SSADM4+ is a further development of the method, part of the commitment to keep it up-to-date with changing technologies and business needs. It is now easier to use, more flexible and customizable. New techniques have been added. It is orientated to finding a solution to a business problem and offers a 'pick and mix' set of tools which can be applied to any type of IT/IS development. The knack is to understand the fundamental purpose of SSADM4+ and which tools help where. This book aims to help.

A look at some of the recent publications shows the spread of SSADM4+'s applicability. SSADM Version 4 was first published in 1990. Since then more than 20 volumes relating to SSADM have been added to CCTA's Information Systems Engineering Library (now maintained and developed as the System Development Library by NCC Blackwell on behalf of the SSADM Management Board). These have included how to use SSADM in environments such as distributed applications, client/server, GUI, re-use and accelerated projects. Interfaces to complementary methodologies have been defined, including the Soft Systems Methodology. Also included is a guide to *Re-use in SSADM using Object-Orientation*. The most recent development has been a major update to the entire method in 1995.

Good Reasons for Using SSADM4+

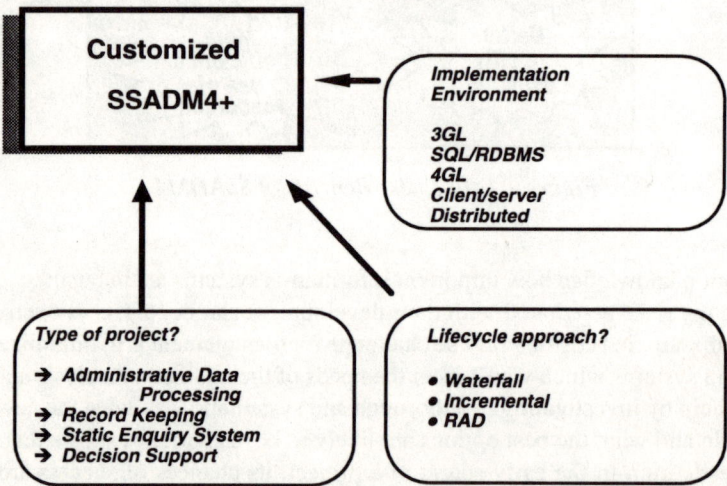

Figure 1.2 Increased applicability of SSADM4+

- **Reducing costs** – SSADM4+ is in the public domain, so no licence fee has to be paid to use any part of it. The only cost is for the purchase of the manuals or the licensing of the hypertext, multi-user edition.

- **Flexibility** – SSADM4+ suits both large and small projects. It fits each project's needs because it is scaleable and tailorable. It is designed to be customized. Whatever the size or type of application, only those elements which are useful to the project are used. If you tailor it to suit your needs, it will provide you with a method which is focused and effective.

- **Reducing risk** – SSADM4+ reduces the risk of project failure. It is the most complete analysis and design method on the market, using well-established techniques to define your business needs. SSADM's proven track record makes it a safe choice.

- **Quality systems** – SSADM4+ is rigorous. Not only does each technique have its own rules, but the method allows you to cross-check the quality and completeness of the deliverables of one technique against others within the method. It involves end-users throughout the analysis and design stage and provides quality criteria against which they can judge all SSADM4+ deliverables.

- **Conforming to standards** – SSADM4+ uses established techniques and is itself an industry standard – BS 7738. It is a good basis for contracts between customers and suppliers.

- **Support** – SSADM4+ is well-supported by documentation, training companies and purveyors of software tools. There is a hypertext edition available for easy browsing and reference at the workstation.

- **Widely known techniques** – This helps to focus advertisements for staff, ensuring that applicants know the specific skills expected of them. Because of the popularity of SSADM4+ there is an extensive skills base available in the market-place. It is also a boost to staff to know that they are being taught and are using modern industry-standard techniques. There are ISEB accredited training and practitioner qualification schemes

- **CASE tools** – All of the techniques within SSADM4+ are supported by CASE (Computer Aided Software Engineering) tools. With CASE tools your documentation is automatically generated as part of the analysis and design process. This not only facilitates the work of the analyst, but also brings the benefits of traceability, cost-effectiveness and quality to your project.

- **User involvement** – SSADM4+ integrates with Business Activity Modelling. It provides information to support operational activities, user job design, measures of performance of business activity, management decisions and control actions. It gives better understanding of business needs by emphasizing the involvement of business users, for example by adding users to the development team or involving them in workshops to define requirements.

- **Future planning** – SSADM4+ is teachable and re-usable. Once staff have used it, the skills and experience can be transferred, thus reducing the learning curve on future projects. SSADM4+ is being continually revised and expanded, increasing its applicability to more and more types of IS project.

- **Usability with other methods and techniques** – An enormous amount of effort has also been expended in providing guidance on how SSADM4+ interacts with the latest techniques in the market-place, such as JAD, prototyping and RAD. See chapter 7 on customizing SSADM4+ for more information.

- **Hardware and software independence** – SSADM4+ avoids a user being locked in to a specific hardware or software environment. It separates the logical design from the physical implementation. This also means that a user can implement the solution on any number of different hardware and software environments without changing the logical design.
- **Project management** – SSADM4+ aids project management with its modularity. It is easy to fit those SSADM procedures which a project needs into a project management structure of controllable stages. It has strong links with PRINCE, the well-established project management method (also in the public domain).
- **Structured approach** – SSADM4+ helps provide a good basis for common understanding when development of IT systems is carried out by third parties.

Key SSADM4+ Features

The key features of SSADM4+ are:

- a System Development Template, defining a broad project structure, a complete framework for the development of information systems;
- provision of IT support for business activity, i.e. being business-led;
- a 3-schema Specification Architecture, which separates the specification and design of the required system into:
  - **Conceptual Model** – The underlying data and business logic which the system needs to contain;
  - **External Design** – The user interface which provides the means of accessing the system functions;
  - **Internal Design** – The physical implementation, management and access of the data.

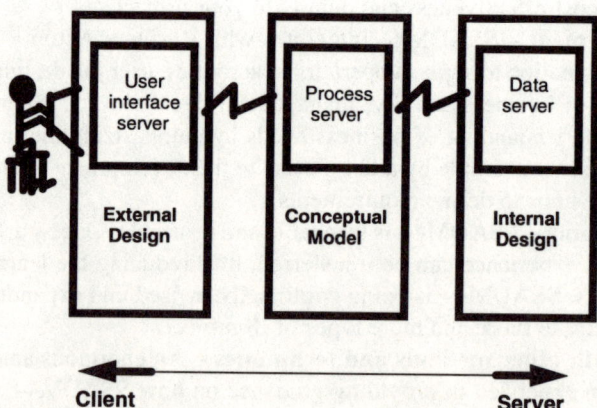

Figure 1.3 Client/server and the 3-schema Specification Architecture

This separation of concerns makes it easier to implement the final system under a variety of hardware and software environments. One type of architecture which matches the 3-schema Specification Architecture very well is the client/server architecture. Client/server architecture proposes that a 'client' process makes a request to a 'server' process which performs a service and sends back a reply. In practice, client processes are often implemented on workstations or personal computers, and server processes are often implemented on a computer which is a resource shared by a number of clients.

A simple mapping of the 3-schema Specification Architecture on to client and server processes means that:

- External Design can be equated to the client;
- Conceptual Model and Internal Design can be equated to the server.

There are many different ways in which the 3-schema approach maps to client/server architecture. For example:

- External Design can be implemented on a user workstation with the Conceptual Model and Internal Design implemented on a mainframe;
- the External Design and Conceptual Model can be implemented on a user workstation with the Internal Design implemented at the database server;
- the External Design and Conceptual Model can be implemented on a user workstation, and Internal Design implemented on a local application server accessing a distributed database.

The 3-schema Specification Architecture is also robust – the user area, the user interface server, the process server, the data server may all change, but the impact of the changes is kept to a minimum by the separation of the three areas.

System Development Template

Today's IT systems are needed for many types of scenario, to meet many sorts of business need. These include the replacement of legacy systems, rapid delivery of a new application and many others. Whatever the need there are important considerations other than 'which techniques should I use?'. SSADM4+ provides a framework, known as the System Development Template, which encompasses all the elements needed for a successful project (see figure 1.4).

The System Development Template is a view of the structure of a development project as follows:

- The Decision Structure shows the involvement of management in selecting from options at a number of critical points during the development.
- The User Organization reflects the mapping of business activities and scheduling constraints onto the organizational structure and the involvement of the user throughout the development process.
- The necessary interfaces with company technical policies and standards are covered in the Policies and Procedures section.

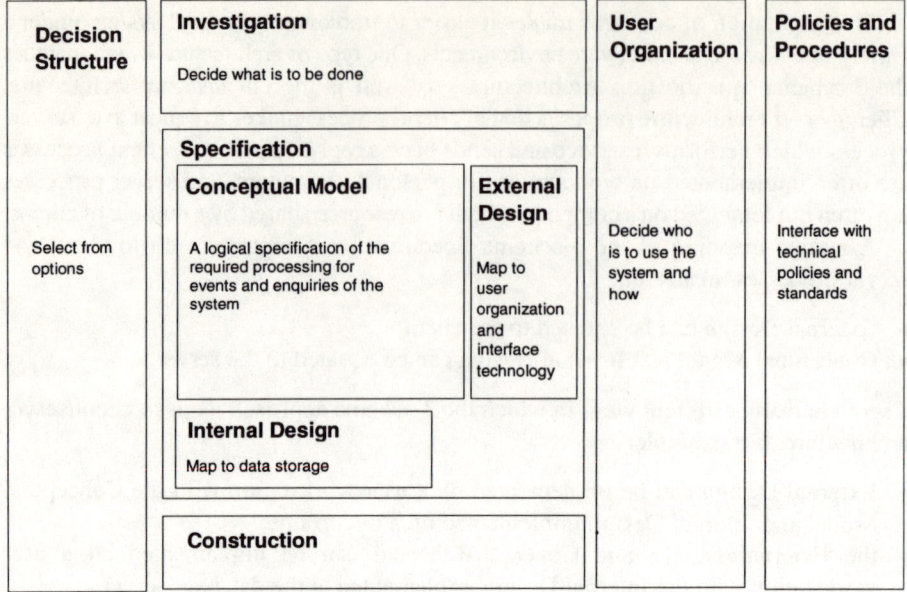

Figure 1.4 System Development Template

- The remaining part of the System Development Template breaks the project down into Investigation, Specification and Construction:
  - Investigation is the early part of a project where the Business Activity Model and the Requirements Catalogue would be created or finalized.
  - The Specification part of a project is a major focus of SSADM4+ where the conceptual services are defined and mapped to the data storage technology and the user organization and interface technology.
  - The Construction part of the project is outside the scope of the core method but is included within the scope of SSADM4+. It includes the development of the system from the design and its testing.

3-schema Specification Architecture

The Specification part of the System Development Template is divided into three separate compartments: the business rules (Conceptual Model); the physical storage and retrieval of data (Internal Design); and the way in which users will communicate with the system (External Design).

Conceptual Model

This comprises the essential business rules and knowledge of the system. It doesn't say how it will be physically implemented. It is independent of both the user interface and the physical database design. It consists of:

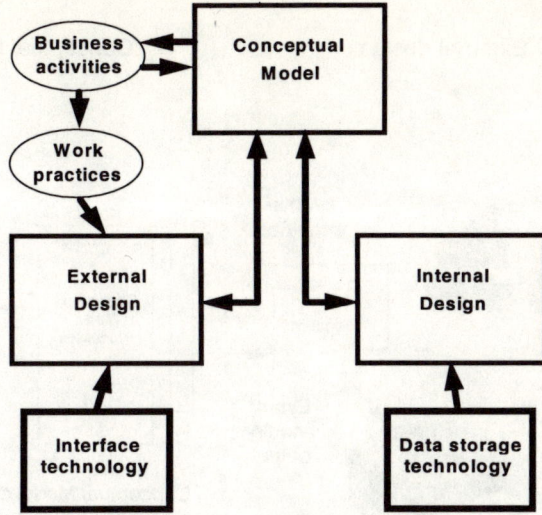

Figure 1.5 Three Distinct Areas of Specification

- A data model – a picture of all the pieces of data, their groupings and interdependencies as the user sees them.
- Enquiry and event processes – the steps and rules to follow to validate, create, modify and delete data, plus the steps to collate the data ready for display.
- Those business activities which are to be automated (or have automated support).

External Design

This comprises the user interface. It has three major elements:

- A packaging of the information from external business activities into suitable submissions to the Conceptual Model.
- Processing specifications:
  - To convert information from business activities to suitable submissions to the Conceptual Model.
  - To convert responses from the Conceptual Model to outputs for users.
- A mapping of the External Design's logical specification to a suitable technology to handle the physical input and output of data.

Internal Design

This defines the physical design of the database and the interface between the processing and the data which is known in SSADM as the Process/Data Inferface (PDI).

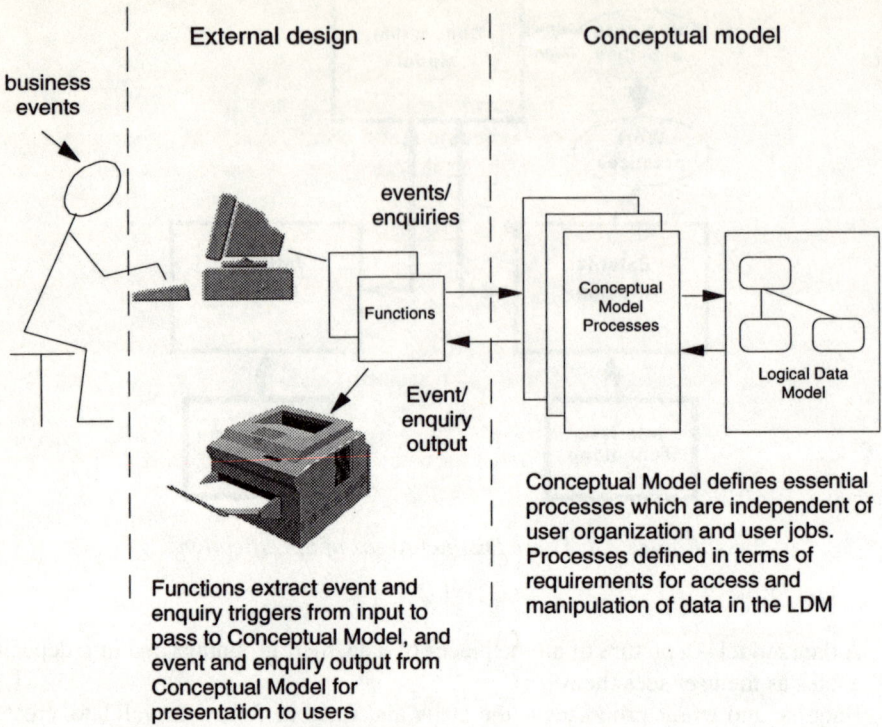

Figure 1.6 External Design and the Conceptual Model

The Fundamental Components of SSADM

SSADM is a complete method which provides a framework, a set of integrated techniques, and a defined set of end-products for the analysis and design of all types of information system. Each project is different and these components will need to be tailored to its needs. This is the customization process. SSADM is designed to be customized. During the process there are three characteristics which must be preserved if the resulting product is to be accepted as essentially SSADM:

- The separation of concerns in the 3-schema Specification Architecture, described above.
- The logical data model – it must have a central, significant role in the development approach.
- The event (for example, the receipt of a new order) – this must be the significant unit of processing specification, from the identification of business activity in analysis to the commit unit in physical design.

Logical Data Model (LDM)

This is represented by a diagram, the Logical Data Structure, supported by documentation which describes the elements of data (entities) and their relationships (for example, the relationship between customers and orders would be 'a customer may place many orders'). The contents of the LDM can be determined from the information needed to support the business activities. This information indicates the events needed to capture that data and also keep it up-to-date. There should be events corresponding to:

- the birth and death of every entity type ('here's a new customer' or 'this product has been discontinued');
- swapping of changeable relationships ('this employee has changed departments');
- making and breaking of optional relationships ('this employee no longer has a company car').

An input or trigger must be available for every type of event identified. The source, within the business, of each input or trigger must also be determined.

Position of SSADM in the Application Development Life Cycle

A project needs a structure if it is to be planned and controlled in a sensible manner. Management, the users and the development staff all have to know how the project intends to progress from identification of the problem to final implementation of a solution if they are to avoid confusion and lack of direction.

There are many different styles of application development, each with its own appropriate life cycle. New styles are being developed each year and there are constant variations on known themes. SSADM's approach to this problem is to provide a basis, the default Structural Model, plus some guidelines and a number of typical examples and expect this to be customized for each new project.

Generally, a SSADM customization strategy will be a component of a broader strategy which affects the way in which projects are undertaken. An overall diagram of the SSADM customization process within a project implementation strategy is shown in figure 1.7. Documentation of the justification for customization is very important. It needs to be explained, for example, why radical customization was required for a particular project. It provides traceability of decisions, an important factor in ensuring control in the method's use and consistency between projects.

Factors Which Influence the Customization of SSADM

SSADM may be customized for the following reasons:

- To respond to specific characteristics of the application to be developed (available technology, type of application).

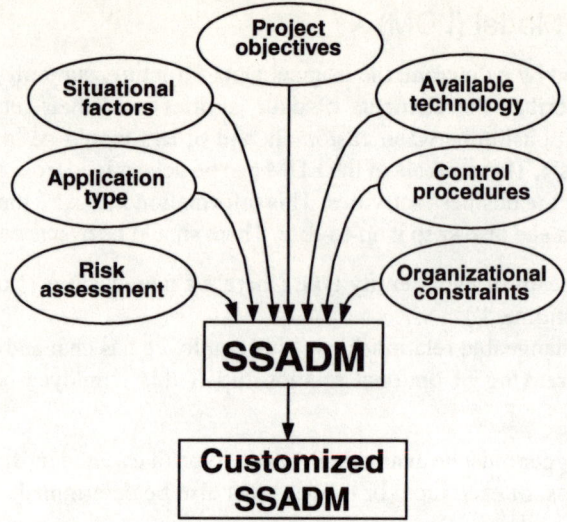

Figure 1.7 Factors influencing customization

- To meet specific constraints (resources, strategies, policies, standards).
- To meet specific concerns about risks (more decision points required).
- To meet specific project objectives (save time, reduce cost).

A Structural Model or route map for a project is essential for planning and estimating, work allocation, progress monitoring and control.

SSADM's default Structural Model has a number of stated and implicit assumptions regarding the development projects on which it is designed to be used. These assumptions are used simply to highlight the need for modifications to be made to the default Structural Model or to the way in which 'standard' SSADM techniques are applied in practice. This customization is a natural part of planning any project. The ability to customize SSADM to the requirements of any project is at the very heart of its rationale. An overview to this customization is given later in the book (chapter 7), but more detailed guidance is available in the System Development Library.

The SSADM Architecture and Products

The SSADM architecture is defined by the System Development Template. This shows that the techniques and activities of SSADM in Investigation and Specification not only lead to the Construction of a system, but require interfaces with:

- a Decision Structure (management decisions and choices);
- the User Organization (work practices, user roles, human interfaces);
- Policies and Procedures (installation standards, hardware strategy, etc.).

Each component of the System Development Template is taken and its relationship to

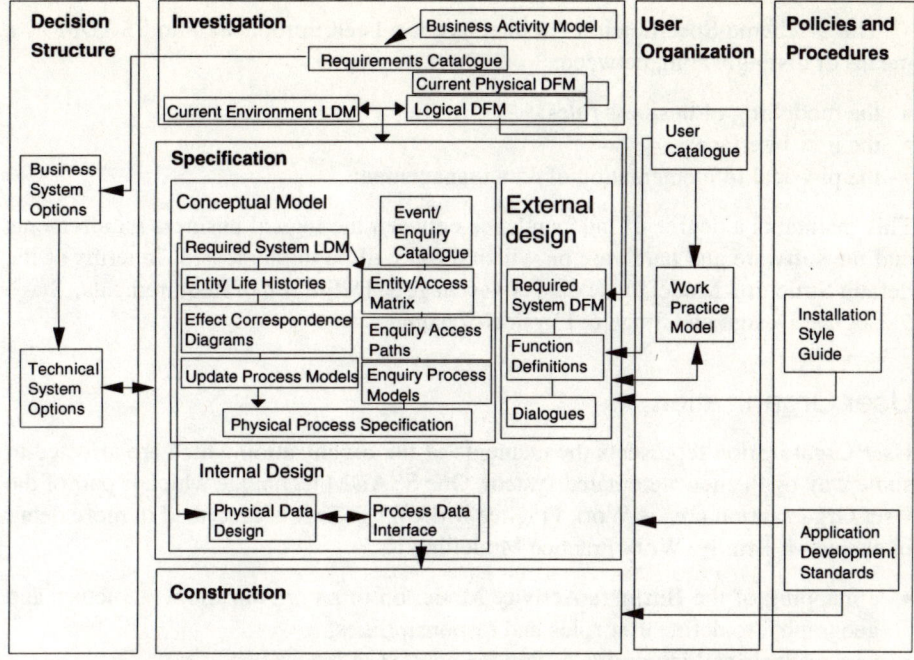

Figure 1.8 System Development Template and SSADM products

the other components, the SSADM products involved and how the SSADM techniques are used is discussed (see figure 1.8).

Investigation

Investigation represents the part of a project which collects as much information as possible on what is required from the new system prior to specifying it in detail. This might involve:

- deriving a model of business activities using Business Activity Modelling;
- developing Data Flow Models;
- developing Logical Data Models;
- building small prototypes to help in eliciting requirements;
- documenting the requirements derived from all of the above.

In terms of SSADM's default Structural Model, Investigation comprises Stage 0: Feasibility and Stage 1: Investigation of Current Environment.

Specification

Specification represents the definition of what needs to be done for a new automated system, based on the results of Investigation. It contains the different components of the 3-schema Specification Architecture.

The 3-schema Specification Architecture has been introduced into SSADM as a means of distinguishing between:

- the modelling of business rules;
- the user interface;
- the physical implementation of data management.

This maintains a degree of independence between the logical business requirements and the software and hardware on which these will be implemented. In terms of the default Structural Model this would cover Stage 3: Definition of Requirements, Stage 5: Logical Design and Stage 6: Physical Design.

User Organization

User Organization represents the elements of the organization which are affected in some way by the new automated system. One SSADM technique which is part of the User Organization area is Work Practice Modelling. This is described in more detail in chapter 4. Briefly, Work Practice Modelling is:

- a mapping of the Business Activity Model on to an organization's structure and geography, to define user roles and responsibilities;
- user analysis and job design within the context of the project.

There is a strong link between the Business Activity Model created in Investigation and the Work Practice Model. The Business Activity Model covers the what, why, when and how of activities. The Work Practice Model covers the who and where.

Part of system design and implementation will need to examine user roles and job descriptions: what they are now and what they will be in the new system. There may be constraints from the end users on changes to their roles and jobs.

Decision Structure

The Decision Structure represents the various points in a project at which user or project management make decisions. There can be a number of formal decision points within a project and these may be tailored to suit the project. The decision points specifically covered by SSADM are:

- acceptance of the Project Initiation Document;
- decision on the Feasibility Report recommendations;
- selecting a Business System Option;
- selecting a Technical System Option.

Policies and Procedures

These reflect the need for a project to interface with the organization or site policies and standards. Among these may be hardware and software strategies or constraints, quality standards, the Style Guide for application designers, staffing policies and policies governing the use of package solutions, in-house development and procurement.

There are a number of procedures which may be required in a project which are not part of analysis and design, but will interface with work covered by SSADM. These include capacity planning, estimation, project management, configuration management and others. The major procedures are described briefly in the annex Project Procedures.

Part II
TECHNIQUES

Techniques Overview

Before examining the SSADM techniques, two messages are worth repeating:

- It is not expected that all SSADM techniques will be needed for every project:
- Where a technique is needed, it may not be necessary to use it to the lowest level of detail and it may not always be used in quite the same manner, i.e. the technique can be tailored.

Every project should be judged on its needs. Bearing in mind the fundamentals described in part 1, use only those techniques which are useful, and use them to the level appropriate for that project.

CASE tools support the major techniques of SSADM and can be of great assistance in its implementation. They can provide automated support of the techniques, automated model transformation (e.g. Effect Correspondence Diagrams into Update Process Models) plus documentation support.

Figure 1.8 on page 13 shows where SSADM products are used in the System Development Template, their typical sequence and interaction. Each of the SSADM techniques delivers one or more of these products.

This is not the full story because many of the techniques can be used in more than one place in a system's development. For example, Data Flow Diagrams can be used to model the current system, a logical view of that system, Business System Options and the required system.

Table 1 on page 20 shows where the techniques can be used in the SSADM stages of the default Structural Model. Together the two figures can help the newcomer to SSADM to get a better feel of the use of the techniques in a project.

	Feasibility	Requirements Analysis	Requirements Specification	Logical System Specification	Physical Design
Business Activity Modelling	■	■			
Business System Options	■	■			
Conceptual Process Modelling			■	■	
Data Flow Modelling	■	■	■		
Dialogue Design		■	■	■	
Entity Behaviour Modelling			■		
Function Definition			■		
Logical Data Modelling	■	■	■		
Physical Data Design					■
Physical Process Specification					■
Prototyping	■	■	■	■	
Relational Data Analysis		■	■		
Requirements Definition	■	■	■		
Technical System Options	■			■	
Work Practice Modelling	■	■	■		

Table 1 SSADM techniques in the default Structural Model

2
Investigation

Business Activity Modelling

Purpose A Business Activity Model explicitly models what goes on in the business which is to be supported by the required information system. Its main purpose within SSADM is to enable the analyst to develop requirements to be added to the Requirements Catalogue directly from the needs of business activities.

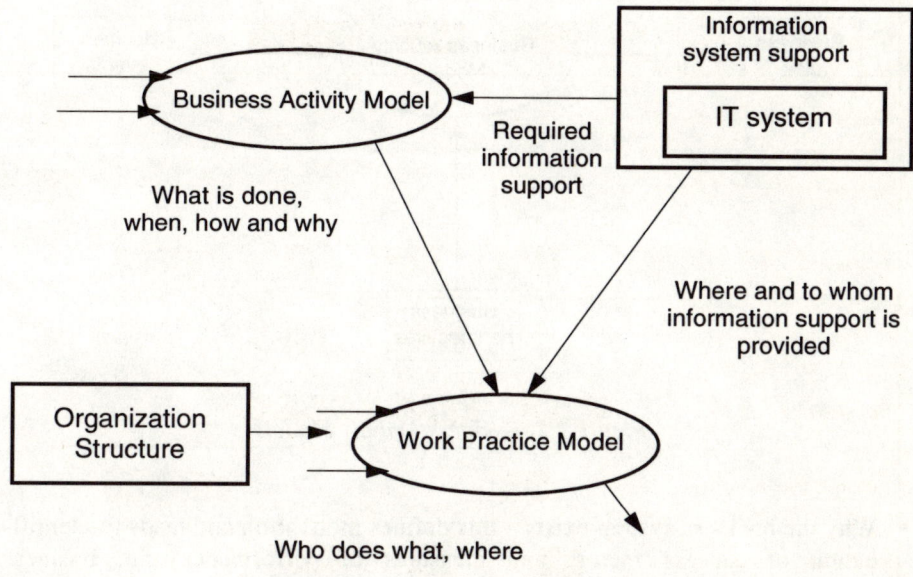

Figure 2.1 Business focus

Overview Business Activity Modelling is undertaken at the beginning of a project – in the Investigation area of the System Development Template. Its activities are independent of the organizational structure and the allocation of tasks to individuals.

21

These are considered in the Work Practice Model. Separation of the Business Activity Model from the Work Practice Model means that, for example, the organization could be restructured, user responsibilities changed and business functions moved to different locations without affecting what the business has to accomplish, as embodied in the Business Activity Model.

SSADM does not mandate a particular method of developing Business Activity and Work Practice Models. There are several methods with which SSADM can work in concert.

The Business Activity Model contains four components:

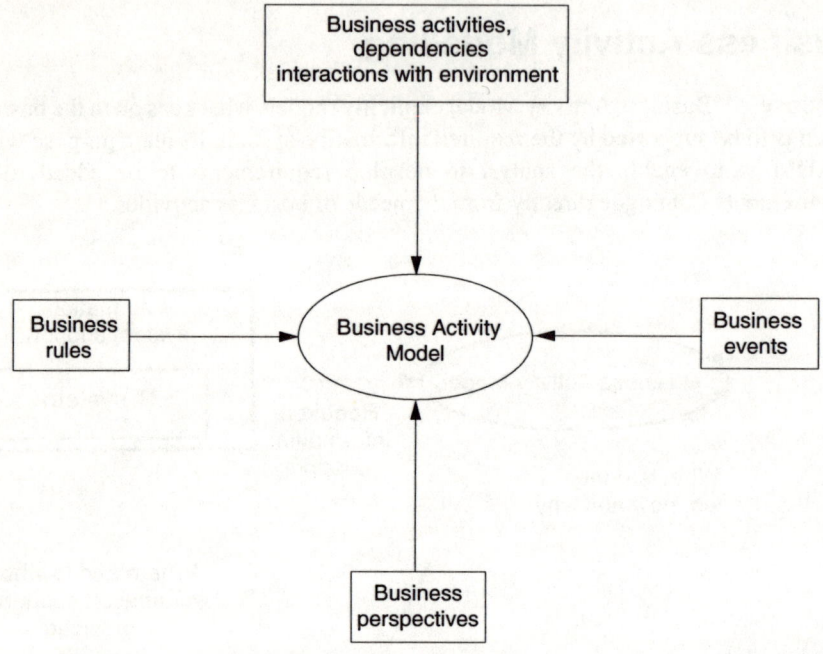

Figure 2.2 Business Activity Model

- Why the business system exists – this defines motivation and leads to identification of success factors and measures of performance, i.e. business perspectives.
- What is done – business activities, the dependencies between them and the resources they use.
- How activities are done – business rules, constraints, calculations, transformations.
- When activities are done – business events which trigger business activities.

A Business Activity Model should be provided as input to the SSADM project or developed at the start of the project.

Relationship to other techniques

Requirements Definition – The Business Activity Model should drive the Requirements Definition in the area of functional requirements. Functional requirements are defined explicitly in terms of information support for business activities.

Data Flow Modelling – Examination of the Current Physical Data Flow Model can lead to the question 'What business activities is this supporting?' The reverse is also true. The Business Activity Model can be used to evaluate the Current Physical Data Flow Model and ask the question 'Is what we are doing now adequate to support the business need?'

Logical Data Modelling – The Business Activity Model will identify the data which should be covered in the Current Environment Logical Data Model and later will help to identify the data needed in the Required System Logical Data Model.

Entity Behaviour Modelling – Identification of the information support needed by the Business Activity Model indicates how data designed in the Logical Data Model is kept up-to-date, and identifies which business activities (events) can provide the inputs.

Work Practice Modelling – This maps the Business Activity Model on to an organization to specify:

- who carries out each business activity;
- where the activities are carried out.

Data Flow Modelling

Purpose Data Flow Modelling is used to investigate and model the flow of data around a system:

- to and from agents external to the system;
- to and from processes which transform the data;
- into and out of repositories or stores of data.

Overview Data Flow Modelling is used in several areas of the System Development Template:

- Investigation, to model the current system and derive a logical view of that system.
- Decision Structure, part of presentations of alternative designs for the new system.
- Specification, the first part of External Design to develop a clear picture of the required system.

The diagrams are easy to understand and therefore provide an effective basis for communications between analyst and user.

Data Flow Model   The main product of Data Flow Modelling is the Data Flow Model. It is composed of five sub-products:

- Data Flow Diagram – Level 1. This represents the whole system on one diagram.
- Data Flow Diagram – Lower Levels. Each process on Level 1 can be decomposed to show more detail in Lower Level Data Flows until the desired level of detail has been reached.
- Elementary Process Descriptions. A brief textual description is written for each process at the lowest level of decomposition.
- I/O Descriptions. A list of the data items contained in each Data Flow which crosses the system boundary.
- External Entity Descriptions. These record any relevant detail about the responsibilities or functions of the external entity, and possible constraints on how it interfaces with the system.

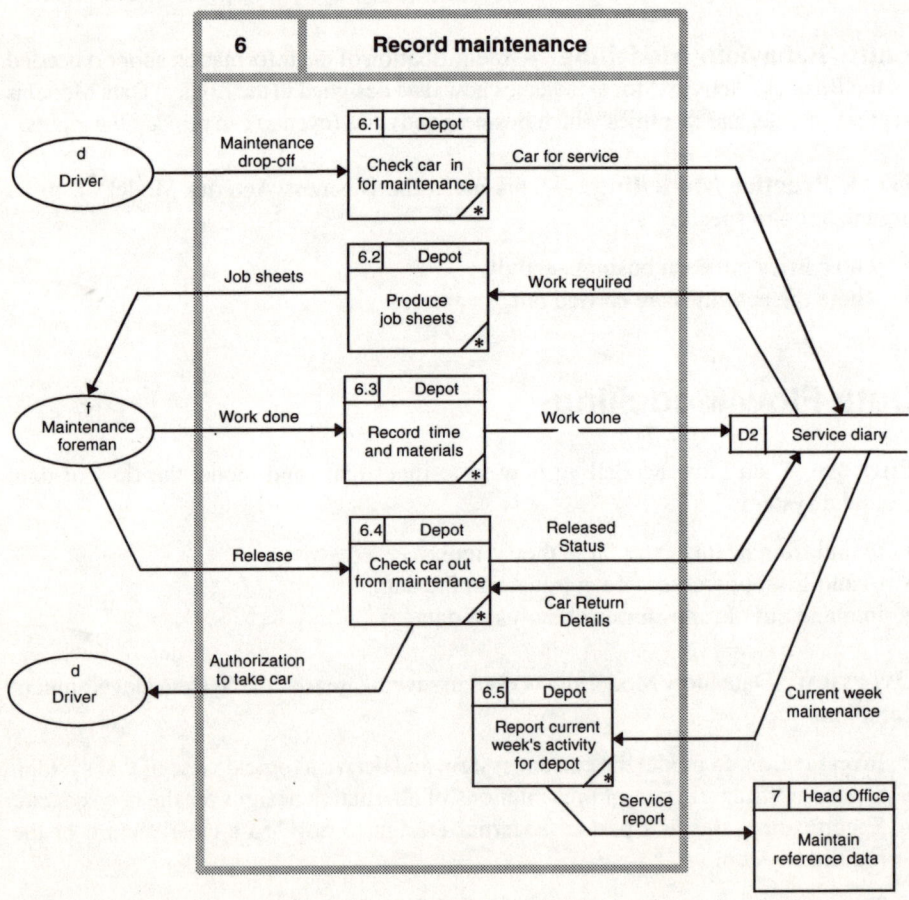

Figure 2.3 Data Flow Diagram example

Figure 2.3 is an example of a Data Flow Diagram in a car maintenance environment. It shows the combination of the symbols and illustrates the ease of understanding the diagrams and how they can be useful in communicating understanding between analyst and user. The items in ellipses, e.g. 'Driver', are external entities. The arrows show information passing between them and the processes (shown in boxes). Alongside each arrow is a description of the information being passed, e.g. 'Car for service'. The open box, 'Service diary', represents data which is stored by the system. The diagonal line in the Driver external entity means that this entity is used more than once in the diagram. The asterisks in the bottom corner of the process boxes mean that they have been taken to the lowest level required.

Logical Data Modelling

Purpose   To produce an accurate model of the data requirements of a system.

Overview   Logical Data Modelling is at the very heart of SSADM, one of the elements which must be included in a project, whatever the customization of the method, if the project is to be able to claim to be using SSADM. It is used in two parts of the System Development Template.

Logical Data Modelling is used to investigate and model the structured data that is held within a system as information support to business activities. The technique is used to model the data of the current system and to build a model of what is required. It shows how the data is logically grouped and those relationships between the groupings which are of interest to the system.

- Investigation – To build the underlying structure of the data which supports the current system.
- Specification – To build a model of the data required to support the new system, which will then be used as the basis for file or database design. Within Specification, Logical Data Modelling forms a key part of the Conceptual Model.

Two different Logical Data Models are produced:

- Current Environment Logical Data Model – To provide a detailed description of the information used or produced by the current environment.
- Required System Logical Data Model – To provide a very detailed description of the information requirements of the new system.

In addition, an Overview Logical Data Model can be produced during Feasibility or Project Initiation.

A Logical Data Model comprises:

- Logical Data Structure;
- Entity Descriptions;
- Relationship Descriptions.

Logical Data Structure   This is a diagram of the logical groups of business data entities and their relationships. Figure 2.4 is an example of a Logical Data Structure for a car hire system.

It shows, for example, that a branch is the owner of many cars; each car is a specification of a car model of a manufacturer. A customer is responsible for one or more rentals, each of which is a request for one car group and one car model.

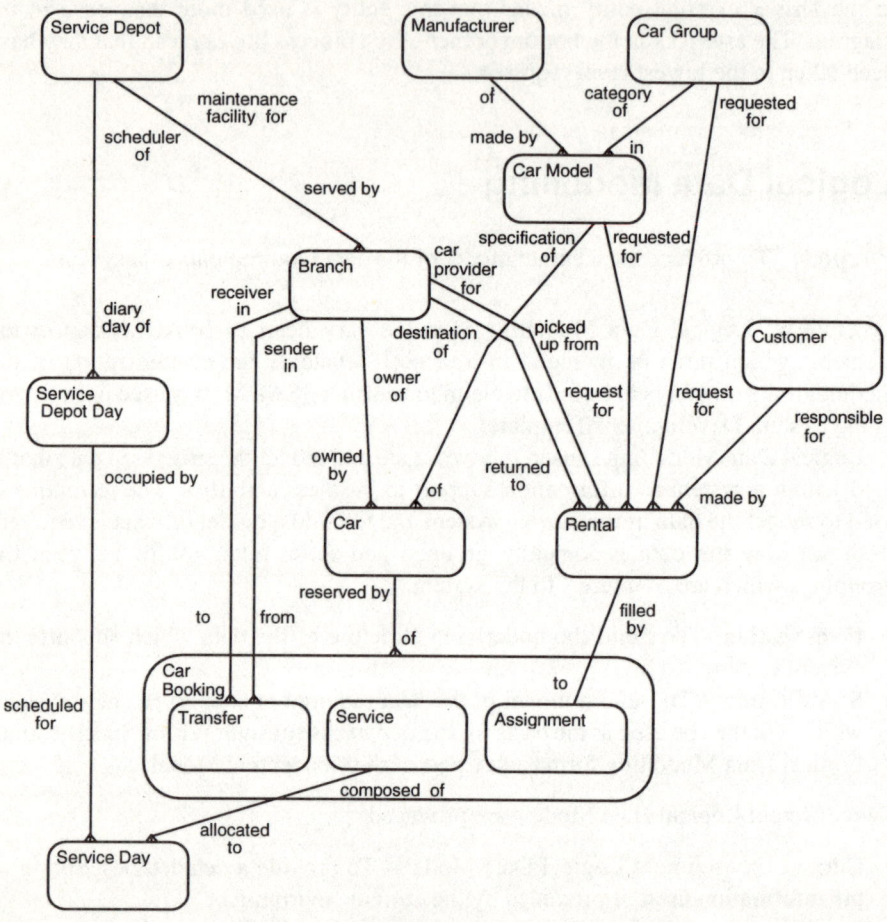

Figure 2.4 Logical Data Structure example

Entity Descriptions   An Entity Description records information about the important characteristics of each entity on the Logical Data Structure. Such information would contain, for example, entity name, average and maximum occurrences, attribute list, user access, ownership and description.

Relationship Descriptions   If the diagram says enough about a relationship, no separate Relationship Description is needed. If more precise volumetric information is needed, this would be put in a Description. Such data might include minimum, maximum and average occurrences or growth per period.

Requirements Definition

Purpose Requirements Definition establishes functional and non-functional requirements for the proposed system. Its objectives are to:

- identify requirements for the proposed system which meet the needs of users and of the business as a whole;
- describe requirements in quantifiable terms;
- provide a basis for decisions about the new system;
- ensure analysis is focused on requirements for the future system.

Its end-product is the Requirements Catalogue, developed in Investigation and used by activities in all other parts of the System Development Template.

Overview The Requirements Catalogue is a key component of SSADM which provides a complete and accurate specification of requirements for the proposed system, and is the basis for design activities.

The Requirements Specification is a composite product containing major parts of the Conceptual Model and the External Design, the interface requirements of the Work Practice Model, and the data management requirements of the Internal Design.

The IT system is developed for support of user jobs – business activities, grouped into tasks, carried out by user roles which are assigned to people in the organization. In general, the IT requirement is derived from the job, not vice versa.

Requirements Definition is iterative, addressing requirements in increasing detail as the project progresses. Deciding how much detail is required at any given point is a matter of judgement rather than formality. Requirements should always be described in terms which:

- can be measured;
- are detailed enough to reduce ambiguity and can be the basis of decisions;
- minimize duplication across the various Specification products.

The Requirements Catalogue The Requirements Catalogue is the central repository for information about requirements, and is a flexible tool for recording and tracking requirements. It is created at the start of Requirements Analysis, or may be provided from an earlier Feasibility Study. Initially requirements may be recorded only in general terms in the Requirements Catalogue. As the project progresses the Requirements Catalogue is extended and refined new requirements are identified and more detail is added.

The Requirements Catalogue is supported by the Business Activity Model and should always be focused on the future, although requirements may be derived from problems in current systems. Current computer systems and manual procedures can

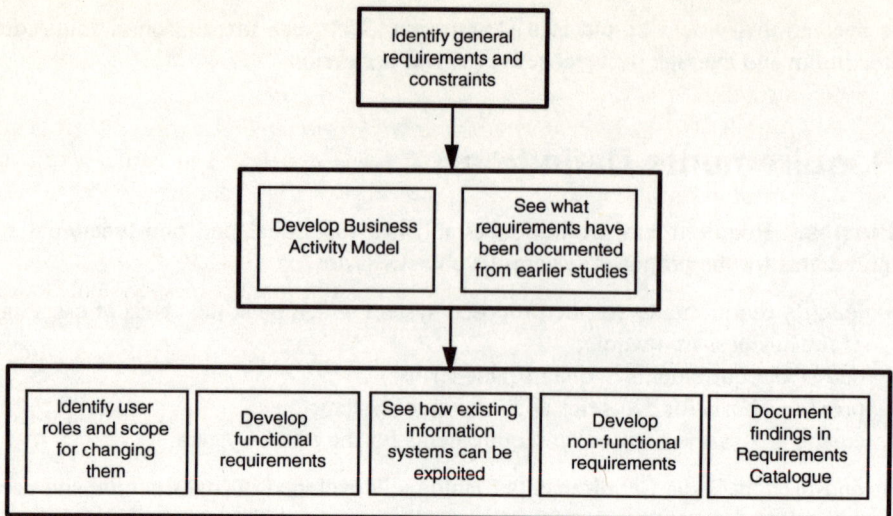

Figure 2.5 Requirements Definition activities

be modelled using the Data Flow Modelling and Logical Data Modelling techniques. Both functional and non-functional requirements are recorded in the Requirements Catalogue.

The activities undertaken in Requirements Definition are illustrated in Figure 2.5 above and described in the following paragraphs.

Identify general requirements and constraints General requirements are global constraints and requirements for the project, such as requirements to conform with corporate standards for dealing with customers and the general public. They might include the need for the project to fit strategic plans for IS development or overall objectives for the business area under investigation.

Develop Business Activity Model The Business Activity Model specifies what business activities need information support. It should identify requirements for support in the following areas:

- Information support for operational activities;
- Obligations on business activities to provide IS updates;
- Communication between business activities;
- Communication with the outside world;
- Potential for automation of some business activities;
- Collection and presentation of performance data;
- Decision support for control action.

Note that not all IS requirements are IT requirements, and that some IT requirements are met with solutions not developed with SSADM, e.g. e-mail and personal products such as spreadsheets. The Business Activity Model's needs for information support are the source of most SSADM functional requirements.

See what requirements have been documented from earlier studies There may be a partially developed Requirements Catalogue developed in earlier work, for example, in a Feasibility Study.

Identify user roles and the scope for changing them The scope for changing user roles is an important factor in Requirements Definition, Business System Options and Work Practice Modelling. Some projects have to provide IT services for user roles which cannot be changed significantly (for example, because user roles are already determined by participation in other systems). The only changes permitted are in the operational detail of how business activity is done and how IT services are used. Requirements will be mainly focused on IT support.

Some projects have authority to redefine user roles to improve work practice (e.g. remove duplicated activity, reduce the number of participants in a business transaction, simplify communication between participants), or maximize exploitation of IT. Requirements will cover both IT support and work practice.

Develop functional requirements Functional requirements are those which define the business processes of the system together with the data required to support them. They provide all the user functions necessary to support the business. They cover the following types of requirements:

- Enquiries;
- Data;
- Outputs of specified form;
- Interfaces with other systems.

See how existing IT systems can be exploited There may be opportunities to use components of existing IT systems by:

- interfacing with them;
- inheriting or migrating their data;
- replacing them, but re-using parts of them such as formats and program modules.

Develop non-functional requirements These are very much concerned with how the future system is to operate in terms of:

- usability requirements;
- service levels;
- performance;
- security;
- audit and control;
- recovery and fallback;

- archiving;
- legislative constraints.

These requirements do not provide any functionality but without their being addressed the new system could prove to be unworkable. Non-functional requirements may be considered to be global in that they stand alone and affect the whole system, e.g. security across a network. Alternatively they may be specific to a particular aspect of functionality, when they would be defined together with the functional requirement. Either way it is essential that these requirements are not overlooked or left until implementation when it is too late to incorporate them into the physical design.

Document findings in the Requirements Catalogue The Requirements Catalogue provides a flexible means of recording and tracking requirements but, since entries are expressed in natural language, it is not sufficient in itself for the precise specification of the required system. A number of more rigorous techniques including Function Definition, Logical Data Modelling and Entity Behaviour Modelling are used to model the required system in detail, drawing on entries in the Requirements Catalogue. The resulting package of products provides a complete specification of requirements.

Some entries in the Requirements Catalogue, such as constraints on the system as a whole and requirements relating to the user interface, are carried forward into the Requirements Specification to be addressed during Logical Design and Technical System Options.

Throughout the project, the analyst must exercise judgement in ensuring that requirements are described in measurable terms and in deciding the appropriate level of detail for each technique, while minimizing duplication across SSADM products.

3

Decision Structure

Business System Options

Purpose The purpose of Business System Options is to describe possible solutions to business needs. Business System Options give the users an initial impression of the possible system solutions they will get; the one they select will form the basis from which the analyst can specify the required system. The description covers the boundary of the system (which functions are included, which are excluded), its inputs and outputs, and indicative costs and benefits.

Overview As this is a Business System Option, not a Technical System Option, it is not concerned with *how* the system will be implemented, just *what* it is to do. A spectrum of options should be developed to allow evaluation of the different combinations and their effect on cost, speed of delivery, organizational impact, ease of use and user satisfaction.

The normal way to approach the creation of options is as follows. One Business System Option should provide a comprehensive solution for every Requirements Catalogue entry. Another should only contain the bare minimum (the mandatory ones and any ancillary functions required by these). A third option would be in between these two. It should attempt to show some of the trade-offs between the low-cost 'minimum' option and the sophistication of the 'maximum' one. Usually three options are sufficient. The final selection is done by the project board or a review panel empowered by the board.

The Business System Option technique

The major output of the technique will be a textual description of the option which includes:

- level of functionality – how well the entire application and its components are intended to function;
- the system boundary, indicating the interface points with the external world;
- volumes, peaks and troughs of data storage required by the option;
- likely time scales for the development of the described option;

31

- approximate Cost/Benefit Analysis;
- impact analysis on existing systems, organization and business;
- training needs;
- any technical considerations which emerge from the option;
- reasons for the selection of this particular option;
- base constraints.

The selected option may be an amalgam of features from more than one of the options put to the project board. The reasons for its selection and any significant reasons for not selecting the other options should be recorded, together with the description of the chosen option. This description should incorporate any changes made to the basic option during the selection process.

Relationship to other techniques

Business System Options are created after the Business Activity Model, Work Practice Model and Requirements Catalogue. They are developed before Requirements Specification.

The text may be supported by Data Flow Diagrams (to show the system boundary), Logical Data Structures and Work Practice Models where this would help the understanding of the option.

A prerequisite to using the technique is that the Requirements Catalogue entries have been prioritized and that it is clear which are the mandatory requirements. The mandatory needs form a list of the minimum requirements which all options must satisfy.

Dialogue Design includes creation of the User Catalogue. This describes the target users and the tasks they do, and is helpful input to the creation of options. Selection of an option may include changes to the User Catalogue.

Prototypes of areas of the proposed system can be developed and demonstrated as part of the formulation and presentation of Business System Options where required.

Technical System Options

Purpose A Technical System Option is a description of how the Selected Business System Option might be implemented. Technical System Options are therefore based on the Selected Business System Option, plus Function Definitions, the Required System Logical Data Model and the Requirements Specification. Their aim is to:

- allow the analyst to picture the entire Business System Option and devise different ways of implementing a solution;
- provide the user with understandable options on possible ways forward and their implications in terms of cost, time-scale and their performance of that part of the user's business.

Overview   One of the major inputs to the formulation of Technical System Options is from the Policies and Procedures of the organization and generally covers:

- technical architecture, including hardware, system software and communications configurations where these items have been determined at a strategic level;
- application architecture, including size, structuring principles, interaction between applications, use of shared data and user interfaces;
- procurement, including preferred hardware/software suppliers, compatibility with existing IT assets and the procedure for procurement;
- organizational standards constraining any of the above;
- the style standards for screen design, mouse and keyboard use, presentation of error messages.

Technical System Options address such areas as:

- a specification of the technical environment;
- confirmation of the functions to be performed and the manner in which they will be carried out;
- impact on the organization;
- impact on the remainder of the project.

The contents of a Technical System Option are listed below:

- **Outline Technical System Architecture (TSA)** – After selection of a Technical System Option the TSA becomes a more detailed stand-alone product. Before that it exists in outline form as part of each Technical System Option. The purpose of the TSA is to provide sufficient information for the user to understand how the system will work, for significant design factors to be explained and for detailed cost estimates to be made. It will cover the required hardware (including network), the target operating system (including network software), any other relevant software environment, the size of the final system and any other significant items, e.g. special fallback and recovery needs.
- **System Description** – A description of how the Requirements Specification is met by the option. The Data Flow Diagrams may be annotated to show how they would be implemented.
- **Impact Analysis** – This describes the impact the option would have on the user business and organization. Any impact on the Requirements Specification is also added.
- **Outline Development Plan** – This defines any required development strategy. This is needed to allow time scales, resource requirements and costs to be calculated.
- **Cost/Benefit Analysis** – A formal Cost/Benefit Analysis is an objective way to judge the merit of one option against another. The major areas which should be covered are:
  - development costs;
  - operating costs;
  - displaced costs;
  - benefits.

Technical System Option technique

The normal sequence of steps is:

- Identify the major constraints.
- Create broad outlines of possible solutions.
- Expand each option with detail sufficient for user management to understand the option and its implications.
- Present, explain and discuss the options with user management.
- Record the decisions and adjust the selected option to reflect those decisions.

Constraints   It is common sense to identify the constraints which will limit the options open to the analyst. These fall into two camps: external and internal constraints.
External constraints include:

- target date;
- maximum budget available;
- mandatory hardware and software;
- the user's organizational considerations (staffing levels, grades, locations);
- the need for the system to achieve business benefits which justify the project.

Internal constraints include:

- interfaces to other systems;
- mandatory facilities;
- performance criteria (service levels) in such areas as:
  - mean time between failures;
  - mean time to repair;
  - availability (usually the on-line hours required);
  - performance (throughput, turn-round);
  - capacity (transaction volume maximums).
- security;
- data storage constraints (from the Required System Logical Data Model) such as:
  - maximum file sizes;
  - backing storage utilization.

Creation of Outline Technical System Options   A number of Technical System Options would normally be created. Although three is a reasonable guide, it may be found that more will need to be considered. Different options should explore candidate technologies for:

- External Design;
- Conceptual Model processes;
- data storage and retrieval;
- communication between Conceptual Model, External Design and Internal Design.

For each option developed it is necessary to ensure that:

- the combinations can work together;
- interfaces to bought-in packages are feasible;
- interfaces to other IT systems are feasible.

Record the decisions The decisions taken at the management presentation should be recorded and the documentation updated to produce the Selected Technical System Option, reflecting the changes and decisions made at the presentation. The TSA of the selected option is updated as part of this final adjustment for input to Physical Design. The selected option should undergo a final capacity planning review to ensure the required service levels can be met.

4

User Organization

Work Practice Modelling

Purpose Work Practice Modelling takes the activities from the Business Activity Model and defines who carries out each activity and where. Work Practice Modelling is:

- a mapping of the Business Activity Model on to an organization's structure and geography to define user roles and responsibilities;
- user analysis and job design within the context of SSADM projects.

Overview There is a strong link between the Business Activity Model created in Investigation and the Work Practice Model. The Business Activity Model covers the what, why, when and how of activities. The Work Practice Model covers the who and where.

The development of a Work Practice Model can be undertaken using the following activities as a guide.

Define the organization structure and user roles In drawing up the organization structure, it is important to find out how stable it is and whether there are plans to reorganize when the new IT system is implemented.

Specify Basic Tasks 'Basic task' here means a group of related business activities to be undertaken by one user in response to one business event. All manual activities triggered by the event can be included in one basic task, unless there are reasons to split it into several tasks. For example:

- Activities may need to happen in different places.
- Activities may need different capabilities or skills.
- Activities may need to be assigned to different people in order to separate responsibilities, to meet audit or control policies.

Each dependency between activities within a basic task needs to be described – does it represent provision of information, provision of some resource, or determine one activity must be completed before another can start?

Specify interactions between tasks Dependencies between activities in different basic tasks also have to be described. This applies to both different tasks for the same business event and tasks for different business events. There may be multiple dependencies and possibly complex interactions between tasks which can be carried out concurrently.

Allocate tasks to user roles Each basic task must be assigned to one or more user roles. Job design skills are needed for this. Co-operation between user roles within business sub-systems should be defined. Also co-operation between business sub-systems should be considered.

Specify interactions between user roles and the IT system There are three types of interaction between user roles and the IT system:

- interaction with automated activities;
- obtaining IT support for manual activities;
- providing input to update the IT system.

The specification of these interactions will be a significant input to the identification of functions in Function Definition and identification of the requirements for dialogue in Dialogue Design. Prototyping may be used to explore the requirements for interaction and there may be some iteration, resulting in reassignment of tasks to user roles and, potentially, changes in the scope of basic tasks.

The second and third types of interaction are determined by the information support requirements of the Business Activity Model. When activities are allocated to user roles, the roles will 'inherit' the enquiries and events associated with those activities.

Allocate user roles to user job descriptions Following this, individual jobs can be designed.

5
Specification

Function Definition

Purpose Function Definition identifies units of processing specification, or functions, which package together the essential services of the system in the way required by the user organization.

Function Definition has several purposes:

- It identifies and defines the units of processing specification to be carried forward to physical design.
- It pulls together the products of analysis and design, which together specify a function.
- It identifies how best to organize the system processing to support the user's tasks.
  - Where the user's job is understood Function Definition will organize the system processing to support these jobs, confirming/revising the design of the user's job.
  - Where the user's job is yet to be defined Function Definition is a more creative activity involving investigation and discussion, assisting in the design of the user's job.
- It develops and confirms a common understanding between the analyst and the user of how the system processing is to be organized.
- It reconciles the two views of the system's processing developed during Requirements Definition as represented in the Required System Data Flow Diagrams and by the events which emerge from Entity Behaviour Modelling.
- It provides a basis for sizing and for deriving design objectives.

Overview Within the System Development Template, functions are the essential building blocks of External Design within Specification. Functions are the mapping of the Conceptual Model on to the User Organization. Regardless of how good the Conceptual Model is, the system will fail if users are not able to access the events and enquiries effectively. A function can therefore be regarded as a 'filter' which extracts event and enquiry triggers from inputs to present them to the Conceptual Model in the right way. In the same way, a function packages up event and enquiry output into user-friendly output.

Function Definition creates the following products:

- Function Description – contains some descriptive text and cross-references to other products.
- I/O Structures – consisting of an I/O Structure Diagram and I/O Structure Element Descriptions, are produced for each function:
  - I/O Structure Diagrams are pictorial representations of those data items input to or output from a function;
  - I/O Structure Element Descriptions are the backing documentation for the diagram. They list the data items represented by each element of the I/O Structure Diagram.

Figure 5.1 shows the relationship between Functions and other SSADM products and techniques.

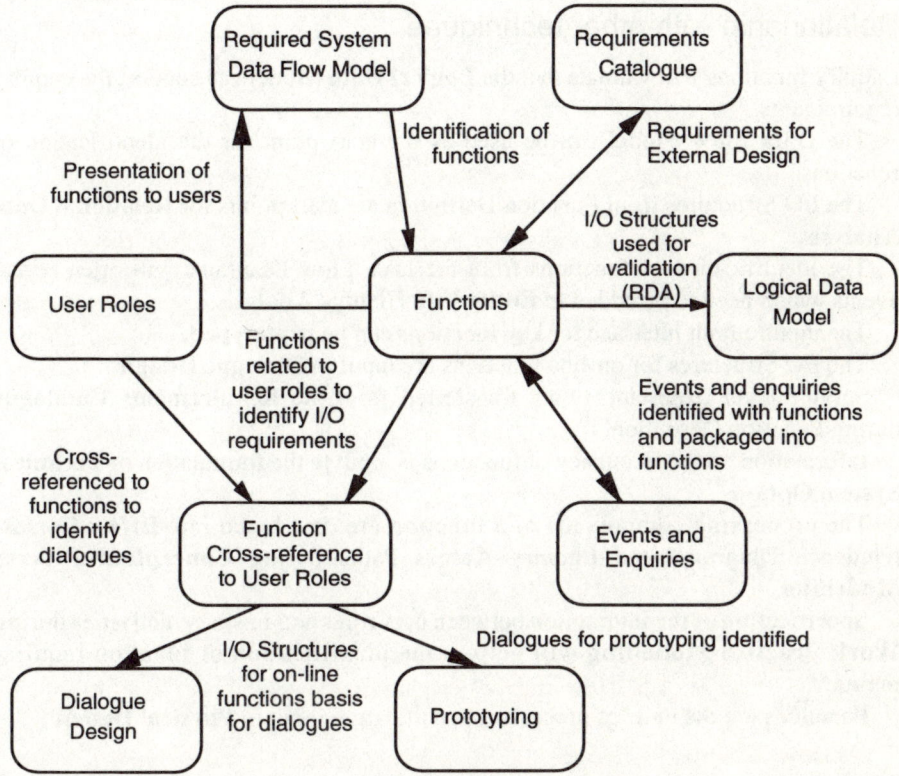

Figure 5.1 Feeds to and from Function Definition

The Function Definition technique

Function Definition is not a technique in the same way as Logical Data Modelling or Entity Behaviour Modelling are techniques. It is not a 'discovery' technique such as

Conceptual Model techniques. Being part of External Design it is more an 'engineering' technique in that an acceptable solution has to be designed and agreed with the user. Functions are a packaging of events and enquiries, and provide the interface between the users and the Conceptual Model.

There are no hard and fast rules to follow to identify functions. The analyst must use skill, creativity and experience to design them.

Function definition consists of the following activities:

- Identify functions;
- Validate the grouping of events and enquiries into functions;
- Rationalize common processing;
- Document functions;
- Produce I/O Structures for each function.

Relationship with other techniques

Enquiry functions will validate that the **Logical Data Model** can support the enquiry requirements.

The **Data Flow Model** can be used as the start point for the identification of functions.

The I/O Structures from Function Definition are start points for **Relational Data Analysis.**

The identification of functions from the Data Flow Diagrams will often reveal events which need to be added to **Entity Life History Analysis**.

The input/output interface for key functions can be **prototyped**.

The I/O Structures for on-line functions are input to **Dialogue Design**.

Service level requirements are transferred from the **Requirements Catalogue** during Function Definition.

Information on the frequency of functions is input to the formulation of **Technical System Options**.

The processing components of a function are developed into Effect Correspondence Diagrams and Enquiry Access Paths during **Conceptual Process Modelling.**

Specification of the interaction between user roles and business activities during **Work Practice Modelling** will help in the identification of function requirements.

Functions are the units of processing specification input to **Physical Design**.

Relational Data Analysis

Purpose   The purposes of Relational Data Analysis are to:

- derive data structures which are free from redundant duplication, unambiguous, and logically easy to maintain and extend;

- capture the user's detailed knowledge of the meaning and significance of the data;
- validate the Logical Data Model by checking that all the required data is present and structured correctly;
- ensure that all data interdependencies have been identified.

Overview The technique is primarily used to enhance and validate the Required System Logical Data Model. It can also be useful in the investigation of the current data for systems which already consist of a large amount of data which are capable of being structured.

The principles of Relational Data Analysis can be used informally to assist in the construction of the Logical Data Model as it is developed throughout the project. The basic principle is that, if organized correctly, all data can be treated as sets of two-dimensional tables of rows and columns.

Table 5.1 All data can be viewed as a set of tables

Cust. no.	Cust. name	Cust. addr.	Credit rating
496	J. Smith	1 High St	1
132	T. Jones	5 North Rd	3
269	M. Green	2 Ridge St	2
504	A. Tutt	6 The Vale	4

If the data maintained for a system contains duplications, this gives the designer problems. Careful records have to be kept of the duplications to make sure that any system enhancements do not let the data get out of step. Relational Data Analysis is a technique for deriving data structures which have the least redundant data and the most flexibility in terms of modification and extension. The motto of Relational Data Analysis is 'keep data only once'.

Relational Data Analysis is a complementary technique to Logical Data Modelling. Logical Data Modelling is a top-down process of identifying the information needed by business processes. Relational Data Analysis derives a data model from the bottom up by examining the data input to and output from the system, and by combining individual data items into larger groups. It ensures that all the low-level detail is captured.

The resultant data groups after the rules have been implemented are called 'normalized' relations. When the Logical Data Model has been modified as a result of Relational Data Analysis it will be a collection of normalized relations. During Physical Design this 'pure' concept of holding data only once may have to be compromised for reasons of speed, but any such moves always make data maintenance more difficult and eventually less flexible.

Relational Data Analysis technique

The technique involves the application of a number of 'normalization' rules to the data groups identified in the Logical Data Model. The rules are:

* Convert the source data into a list of attributes;
* Put repeating groups of data into separate structures;
* Put fields which are only dependent on part of the key into separate structures;
* Put fields which are dependent on other non-key fields into separate structures;
* Combine structures with identical keys.

Entity Behaviour Modelling

Purpose   Entity Behaviour Modelling covers a set of techniques which model the interaction between data and processes in the Conceptual Model. There are three techniques:

* Event identification;
* Enquiry identification;
* Entity Life Histories.

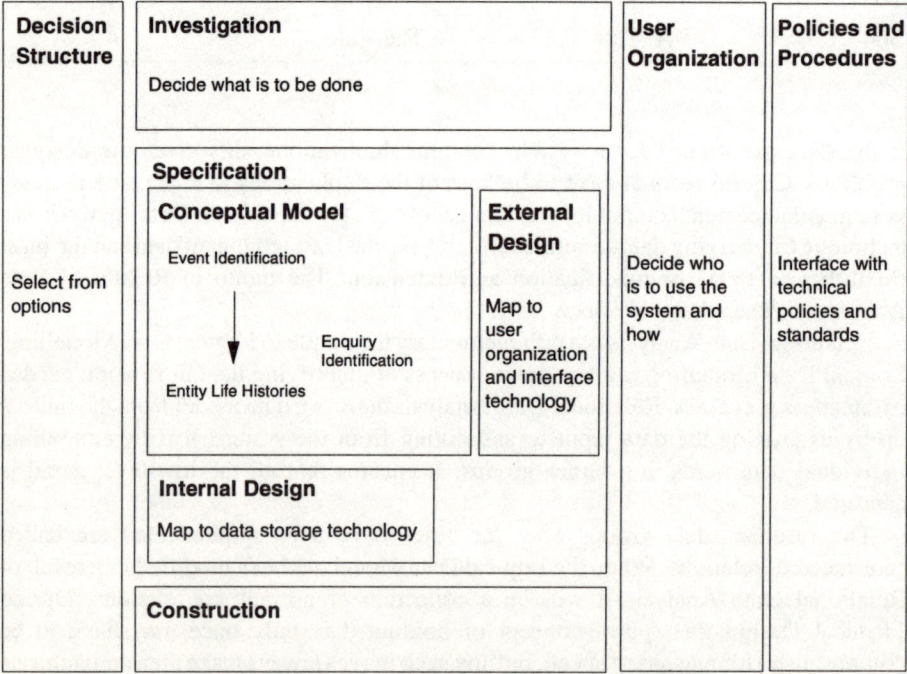

Figure 5.2 Entity Behaviour Modelling techniques

Overview   Events and enquiries are the building blocks for the specification of processing for the required system. Events and enquiries are the triggers to processes in the Conceptual Model which navigate and manipulate data within the Required System Logical Data Model. Events and enquiries are packaged together by functions. Functions act as a filter between users and events/enquiries in the following way:

- Functions extract event and enquiry triggers from user input and pass them across to the Conceptual Model.
- Functions receive the event and enquiry output and format it for presentation to the user.

Event Identification   is a technique which identifies all events by examination of the Required System Data Flow Model and Required System Logical Data. The identification of events can be done in parallel with the identification of functions. Functions can in turn help to identify events. Business Activity Models will also help in the identification of business events which may correspond to events which cause changes to the Conceptual Model data.

Enquiry Identification   is a technique which identifies enquiries by examining the information support requirements for business activities and from user requirements. Knowledge of the enquiries helps to build and validate the Logical Data Model.

Products of Entity Behaviour Modelling

The products which are described in this part of Entity Behaviour Modelling are as follows:

- Entity Access Matrix;
- Event and Enquiry Catalogue;
- Entity Life History.

The Entity Access Matrix, Event and Enquiry Catalogue, and Entity Life History products are described further in the following paragraphs.

Entity Access Matrix

The Entity Access Matrix is a powerful working document that helps to identify which entities are affected or accessed by a particular event or enquiry. As the Conceptual Model is developed, the Entity Access Matrix is built up showing which entities are affected by each enquiry and event.

Entities from the Required System Logical Data Model are placed along one axis of the matrix and events and enquiries are placed along the other axis as they are discovered. Intersections of the matrix are completed to indicate the type of access. If an event accesses an entity in several different ways (possibly in different contexts) several entries can be made in a single intersection of the matrix. Super-events and common enquiries identified during Entity Behaviour Modelling are documented on the Entity Access Matrix as well as events and enquiries.

There are no specific notational conventions for an Entity Access Matrix: the precise format will depend upon the tools available to the project. An example is given in table 5.3.

ENTITIES *EVENTS/ ENQUIRIES*	*Car Booking*	*Car Booking: Transfer*	*Car Booking: Assignment*	*Branch*	Λ *Car*	*Car Model*
EVENTS:						
Car Allocation to Rental	I, T		I, T		G	R
Rental Pick-up	M		M			
Rental Return	M		M	G, L	M, T, C	
Transfer Pick-up	M	M		X	M, S	
Walk-in Rental	I, T		I, T		G	
Car Model Death					D, C	D, C
Car Model Removal						
Car Group Removal						
ENQUIRIES:						
Car Avaliability					R	R
Customer History	R			R	R	R
Unallocated Bookings	R			R		R

Table 5.3 Entity Access Matrix example

The key to the entries in the intersections of the matrix is as follows (note that not all of these categories will be required for all projects):

- **Insert** – This is only used for events. An 'I' indicates that an occurrence of this event causes the insertion, or creation, of one or more occurrences of this entity.
- **Modify** – This is only used for events. An 'M' indicates that an occurrence of this event causes attributes to be changed within one or more occurrences of this entity.
- **Death** – This is only used for events. A 'D' indicates that an occurrence of this event causes the death of one or more occurrences of this entity (i.e. the entity occurrences have no further active role to play in the system but they are still available for enquiries).
- **'Buried' (delete)** – This is only used for events. A 'B' indicates that an occurrence of this event causes the deletion of one or more occurrences of the entity (i.e. the entity occurrences are no longer recognized by the system).

- **Gain detail** – This is only used for events. A 'G' indicates that an occurrence of this event causes one or more occurrences of a detail entity to be linked via a relationship to one or more occurrences of this entity. A 'G' should always have one or more corresponding 'T' entries for the associated detail entities.
- **Lose detail** – This is only used for events. An 'L' indicates that an occurrence of this event causes one or more occurrences of a detail entity to be detached from one or more occurrences of this entity by the severance of relationships. An 'L' should always have one or more corresponding 'C' entries for the associated detail entities.
- **Tie** – This is only used for events. A 'T' indicates that each occurrence of this event causes one or more occurrences of this entity to be linked to an occurrence of a master entity via a relationship. This would be represented by the assignment of a value to the foreign key. A 'T' may have one or more corresponding 'G' entries for the master entities.
- **Cut** – This is only used for events. A 'C' indicates that each occurrence of this event causes one or more occurrences of this entity to be detached from an occurrence of a master entity by deleting a relationship. This would be represented by assigning 'null' values to the foreign key. A 'C' may have one or more corresponding 'L' entries for the master entities.
- **Swap detail(s) between occurrences** – This is only used for events. An 'X' indicates that an occurrence of this event causes occurrences of a detail entity to be swapped from one occurrence of this entity to another by the severance of one relationship and the creation of another relationship. An 'X' may have one or more corresponding 'S' entries for the detail entities.
- **swap master(s) between occurrences** – This is only used for events. An 'S' indicates that each occurrence of this event causes one or more occurrences of this entity to be detached from one occurrence of a master entity and attached to another occurrence of the master by deleting and creating relationships. This would be represented by altering values of the foreign key. An 'S' may have one or more corresponding 'X' entries for the master entities.
- **Read** – This is used for events and enquiries. An 'R' indicates that each occurrence of this event or enquiry accesses one or more occurrences of this value or occurs as part of a navigation path around the Logical Data Model.

This matrix is the primary input to Conceptual Process Modelling. It is also used as an aid to ensure that all events and enquiries are represented in the External Design, and may be used in partitioning the system, for example for a distributed system or to define sub-systems that are to be developed separately.

Event and Enquiry Catalogue

The product within SSADM which may be used to document events and enquiries is the Event and Enquiry Catalogue. Events and enquiries are cross-referenced to entities on the Required System Logical Data Model using the Entity Access Matrix.

The Event and Enquiry Catalogue records information about the important characteristics of each event and enquiry. The Event and Enquiry Catalogue is likely to be in the form of a report from a CASE tool, so it is not possible to be precise about its format or content. Instead, the Event and Enquiry Catalogue is described in terms of the information that needs to be recorded. This information should be available to analysts from whatever tools are used within the project.

Super-events and common enquiries should also be documented in the Event and Enquiry Catalogue and cross-referenced to their corresponding events and enquiries.

It should be noted that some of the information listed below duplicates information that is present on the Entity Access Matrix, Entity Life Histories, Enquiry Access Paths and Effect Correspondence Diagrams. If a CASE tool is available that captures information from these other products automatically, this information does not need to be recorded separately but should still be available for interrogation. The Event and Enquiry Catalogue is simply a view of the information collected by the CASE tool.

Entity Life History

An Entity Life History is a diagram which charts the life of an entity within a system from birth to death in terms of the events which affect it. It is a model of what can happen to an entity over time, and is read from left to right in chronological order of events. This is done in order to define constraints on the updating of entities, and to explore the required degree to which business events and business rules are reflected in requirements for updating data within the system. The results of Entity Life History Analysis are fed into Conceptual Process Modelling.

Entity Life Histories use Jackson-like notation with sequences, selections, iterations and parallel structures as the basic components. Operations can be added to the bottom boxes of the structure (effects). State indicators are added below these to indicate the status of the entity at any point in its life.

A simple example of an Entity Life History for the rental of a car is shown in figure 5.4 to give the reader an idea of what they look like and how they display their information. A rental is shown to have a start, followed by extensions and finishing with the rental return. The start of a rental may be a customer walking into the rental office or an advance reservation. There may be any number of rental extensions.

State Indicators

Each entity has a State Indicator whose value is updated each time an event causes an update to the entity's data. Inspection of the state indicator value of an entity occurrence at any one time will identify where the entity occurrence is within its life, and determine which event(s) may next update the entity occurrence.

The state indicator notation on an Entity Life History is generally of the format 'number(s)/number' where:

- the numbers prior to the slash identify the permitted values of the state indicator prior to its update by the relevant effect;
- the number after the slash represents the value of the state indicator once it has been updated by a particular effect.

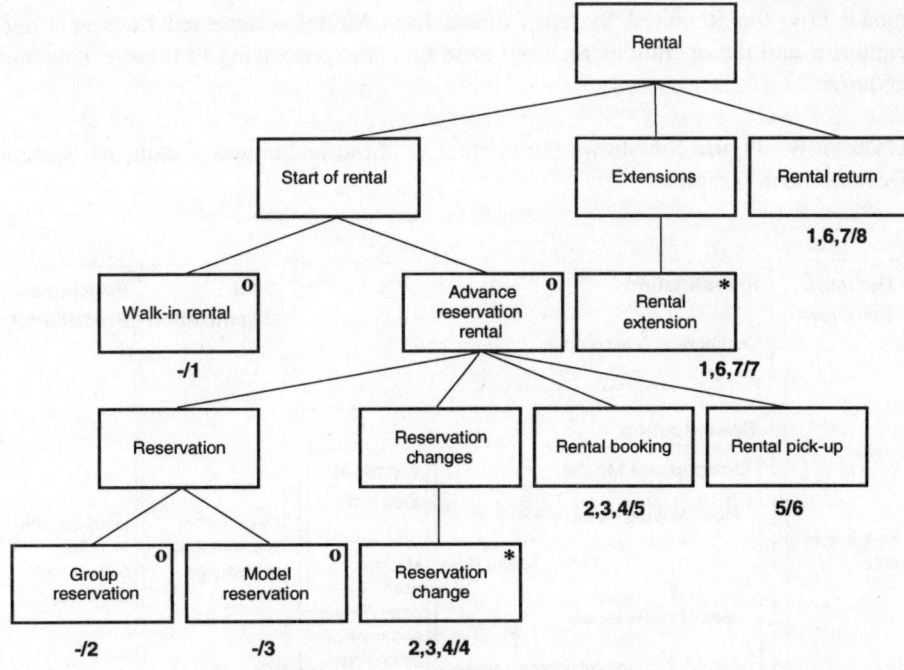

Figure 5.4 Entity Life History example

If in checking the state indicator, the current value is not equal to one of the values of the prior permitted states, the effect cannot take place and exception processing can be invoked.

Figure 5.4 shows the 'life' of a car rental. In the example used, the State Indicators under the box 'Rental Return' are '1,6,7/8', meaning that before the effect 'Rental Return' can be carried out, there must have been any of the following:

- A walk-in rental which set the State Indicator to '1'.
- A rental pick-up which set the State Indicator to '6'.
- A rental extension which set the State Indicator to '7'.

As long as the State Indicator was one of these acceptable values, the effect 'Rental Return' would be carried out and the State Indicator changed to '8'.

The validation logic implicit in the state indicators can be carried forward into logical design and built into the processing logic. However, it is not always desirable to implement state indicators directly in the physical system.

Conceptual Process Modelling

Purpose   Conceptual Process Modelling defines the processing required in response to events (which change or create data) or enquiries. It covers a set of techniques which model how the Required System Logical Data Model is accessed by events and enquiries and the operations required to support the processing of those events and enquiries.

Overview   Figure 5.5 shows the context of these techniques within the System Development Template.

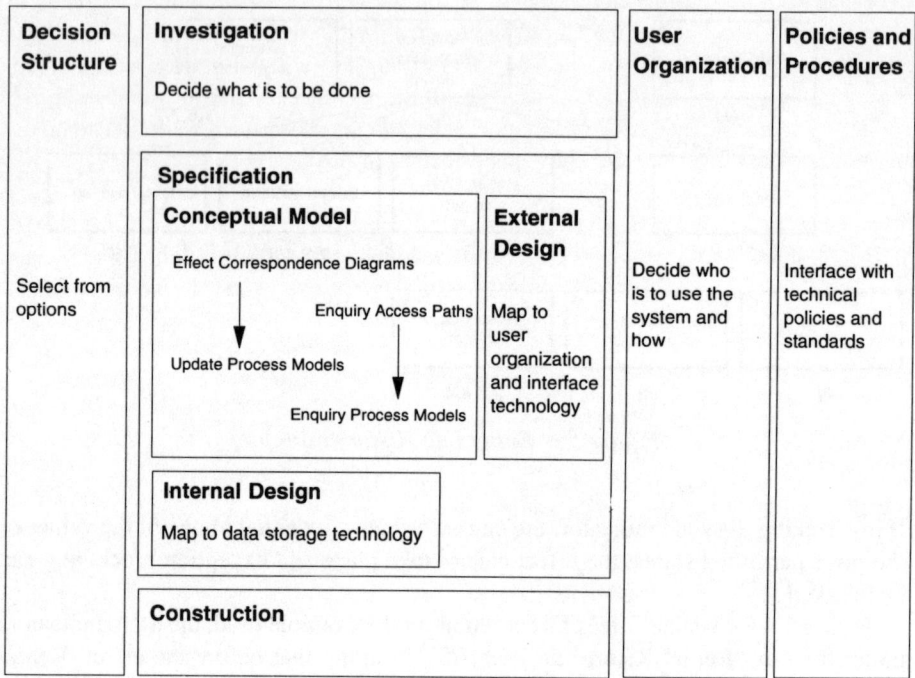

Figure 5.5 Conceptual Process Modelling techniques

The purposes of each of the individual techniques are described as follows:

- Enquiry Access Paths:
  - validate the Required System Logical Data Model by testing it against requirements for information support to the business;
  - specify enquiries in an unambiguous way;
  - create structures for enquiry processes.
- Effect Correspondence Diagrams provide similar structures for update processes.
- Enquiry Process Models transform Enquiry Access Paths into design structures which are suitable for use in Physical Design.
- Update Process Models transform Effect Correspondence Diagrams into design structures which are suitable for use in Physical Design.

Enquiry Access Paths

Purpose   Each enquiry must have an access path through the Logical Data Structure to find the data which it needs. An Enquiry Access Path may be drawn for each enquiry where there is a need to validate that the Required System Logical Data Structure can support the enquiry.

Overview   The Enquiry Access Path technique consists of drawing two types of diagram. The first is an extract from the Logical Data Structure showing only those entities involved in the enquiry. The second diagram is the Enquiry Access Path, showing the type and sequence of accesses of these entities to perform the enquiry.

Only the three structures of sequence, selection and iteration are used. The boxes are joined by arrowed lines to show the direction of the access path.

Selection structure   Many enquiries are based on parameters or selection criteria, for example, an enquiry to find priority 1 customers with cars more than three years old. The selection structure is used to show both the selection of priority 1 customers and the breakdown of car entities into those with a date attribute which meets the selection criterion and those which don't.

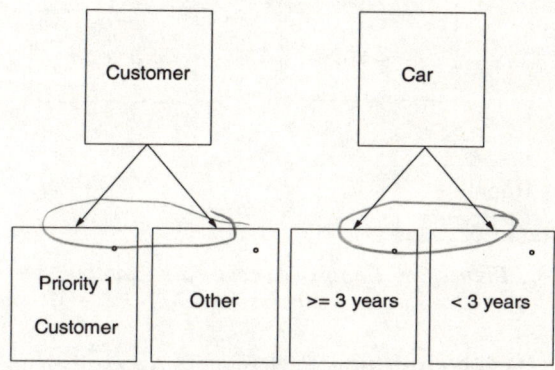

Figure 5.6 Selection example

Iteration structure   If an enquiry has to check each entity in the database against a selection criterion, such as in this example, the iteration structure is used to indicate this (see figure 5.7). The complete Enquiry Access Path for the example would look like figure 5.8.

The initial arrow into the 'set of cars' box shows the entity at which the enquiry begins. The names next to the arrow are those of the attributes whose value will be used as parameters for the enquiry. So the diagram shows that the enquiry begins against the car entity and uses the car purchase date as the search attribute. Where a car meets the requirement, the appropriate customer record is examined for the priority code.

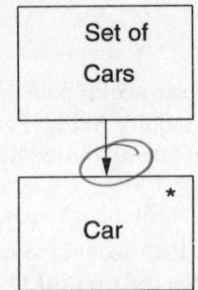

Figure 5.7 Iteration example

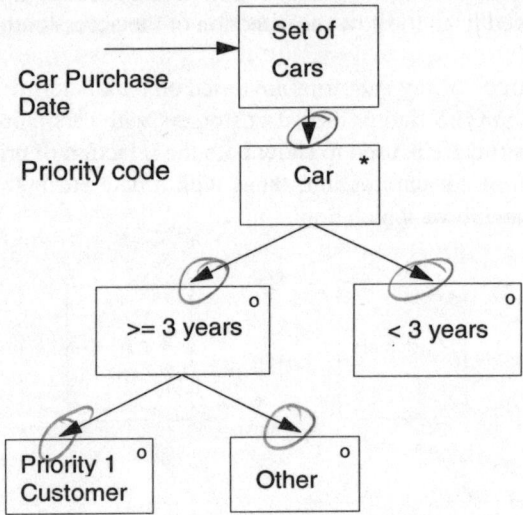

Figure 5.8 Enquiry Access Path example

Enquiry Access Path technique   Each Enquiry Access Path must have a unique name: the name of the enquiry. There are seven basic steps:

Define enquiries   Enquiries are identified from the information support needed by business activities. For each enquiry it is necessary to identify the data items required as output. Enquiry triggers are the parameters necessary for the system to identify the required information. These are often the selection criteria for the entity nominated as the entry point for the enquiry. In the earlier example no key was entered, just the two criteria of priority code and car purchase date.

Identify the entities to be accessed   By looking at the data required for output it is possible to identify which entities must be accessed. If any data cannot be derived from the Logical Data Model, this must be resolved before continuing.

Produce the required view of the Logical Data Structure The Logical Data Structure is either annotated or a separate diagram is drawn which includes the entities identified in the previous step and shows the relationships between them which will indicate the paths to be followed by the enquiry.

Develop initial Enquiry Access Path The Logical Data Structure extract is redrawn using Jackson notation to form the Enquiry Access Path.

Add entry points The key or non-key attributes used for entry next to the arrow to the entry point are listed.

Check Logical Data Model and add operations It is ensured that the designated users of the enquiry have the necessary access rights through the path. This should have been documented in the Entity and Attribute Descriptions. Operations are added to the structure.

Document entry points on the Logical Data Model In order that physical data design can be carried out, all the entry points to the Logical Data Model need to be identified. These can be shown diagrammatically as arrows pointing to the relevant entities, annotated with the relevant data items on the Required System Logical Data Structure diagram.

Effect Correspondence Diagrams

Purpose Effect Correspondence Diagrams show all entities affected by a given event and how those effects correspond with each other. They are used to validate the Entity Life Histories from which they are derived and provide the basis for later, more detailed process specification.

Overview This technique is useful in the case of complex Entity Life Histories. Effect Correspondence Diagrams are equivalent to the Enquiry Access Paths developed during preparation of the Logical Data Model. An Enquiry Access Path traces the path of an enquiry, while an Effect Correspondence Diagram traces the path of an update.

The prime purpose of Effect Correspondence Diagrams is as an input to logical database process design as the basis for the development of Update Process Models. For each event identified in Entity Life Histories an Effect Correspondence Diagram is drawn. This also helps to validate the Entity Life History. For example, the event may be the placing of a new order by a customer. The Effect Correspondence Diagram would discover if all the needed data was available and accessible.

Effect Correspondence Diagram technique The structures used in Effect Correspondence Diagrams are based on the Jackson notation used elsewhere in SSADM. The technique uses selection and iteration structures:

Iteration structures – The iteration structure is required when the event causes more than one entity occurrence to be updated.

Selection structures – The selection structure is required when an event has an effect on a single entity occurrence in two or more mutually exclusive ways.
The steps in deriving an Effect Correspondence Diagram are:

- **Draw a box representing each entity affected by the event**   Examine the Entity Life History and draw a box for each entity affected by the event.
- **Add all effects of events**   All the different effects of this event on these entities are added to the diagram. If there are alternative effects of the event on an entity, create a selection on the Effect Correspondence Diagram under the entity box. If there are simultaneous effects, create a separate box for each effect.
- **Identify entry point**   The entry point is defined as the first entity to be selected, using the input data.
- **Define correspondences**   Correspondences are identified as one-to-one relationships between effects. Each correspondence should ideally relate to a relationship on the Logical Data Structure. Working from the entry point, define correspondences between effects.
- **Deal with iterations**   If an entity is affected by an event in more than one iterative way and access to the entity is by the same relationship, then the effects should be merged into a single structure.
- **Add conditions to selections and iterations**   The condition should state the circumstances under which the option will be chosen or the iteration will be executed. It is not necessary to add conditions to iterations where a complete set of entity occurences is to be accessed.
- **Add operations**   The entry point of the event is shown by a single headed arrow against the first entity to be accessed. List the event data against this arrow. These are the attributes presented by the event, and will normally include a key and attributes carrying update information.

Enquiry Process Models

Purpose   Enquiry Process Modelling is an optional technique which creates a design in diagram form of a program to handle an enquiry. It transforms an Enquiry Access Path into a Jackson program structure with listed and allocated operations ready for use in Physical Design.

Overview   The technique uses the following steps:

Group accesses on the Enquiry Access Path   Any accesses which are in a one-to-one correspondence on the Enquiry Access Path diagram are grouped.

Convert to Jackson-like notation All elementary and grouped accesses become boxes in a Jackson structure.

List the operations and allocate them to the structure The operations come from the Enquiry Access Path.

Allocate conditions to the structure Conditions are allocated for each selection and iteration.

Check the structure The structure conventions for both Enquiry and Update Process Models are shown in figure 5.9. The top box of the structure contains the name of the event or enquiry. The structure contains the following components:

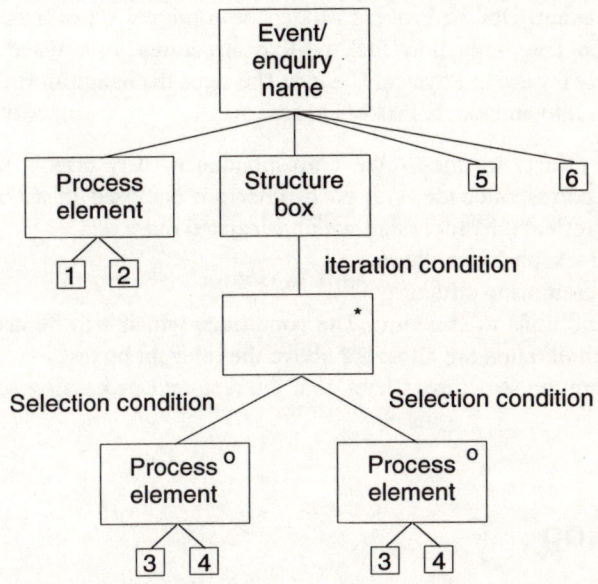

Figure 5.9 Enquiry and Update Process Model conventions

- **Sequence** – represented by a box with a series of plain boxes below it. The sequence of the plain boxes should be read from left to right.
- **Iteration** – represented by a box with a single box below it containing an asterisk in the top right-hand corner. The process represented by this box can be repeated a number of times from zero to many.
- **Selection** – represented by a box with a series of boxes below it containing 'o' in the top right-hand corner. These boxes are alternatives for one another, only one of which will be selected at this point in the structure (if one of the boxes is a 'null'

selection, indicated by a dash, then it is possible for none of the alternatives to be selected).

Operations are added to the boxes in the structure in the sequence in which they are to be carried out.

Update Process Models

Purpose Update Process Modelling is an optional technique which creates in diagram form a design of a program to handle an event, i.e. showing how data will be added, deleted or changed in the Logical Data Model.

Overview An Update Process Model is similar to an Enquiry Process Model, but is used for an event. Update Process Models are optional transformations of Effect Correspondence Diagrams into Jackson-like structures with listed and allocated operations ready for use in Physical Design. The steps to change an Effect Correspondence Diagram into an Update Process Model are:

- Group any effects in one-to-one correspondence. Any effects which are in a one-to-one correspondence with each other are enclosed in a box. The box is renamed to reflect the processing which is carried out.
- Convert to Jackson-like notation.
- Allocate operations to structure.
- Allocate conditions to structure. The conditions which will be used to test each selection and iteration are allocated above the relevant boxes.
- Walk through the structure. Check that the resultant processing sequence makes sense.

Prototyping

Purpose Prototyping has four principal purposes:

- To establish or clarify requirements for the new system.
- To obtain feedback from the users on the possible look and feel of the new system.
- To demonstrate the usability of the Conceptual Model.
- To compare different approaches.

Overview A prototype is a model or example of something, used to help envisage the finished article during the design process. Prototypes are usually in the form of screens and menus with limited underlying functionality, developed as a basis for agreement between user and developer. In SSADM prototypes are used for a specific purpose and then thrown away.

Prototyping is not:

- an alternative method to SSADM;
- in itself a Rapid Application Development approach, although it is a major component of most RAD methods.

Types of Prototyping There are four types of prototyping, one for each of the purposes mentioned:

- **Requirements** – This is to clarify requirements and elicit further requirements. It may be done at any time before Physical Design.
- **Demonstration** – This demonstrates the look and feel of the new system to obtain feedback from the users. The results may be used to develop the style guide for the new system. It is usually done in Investigation.
- **Specification** – This type aims to demonstrate which parts of the system are workable and which are not. It is done in Specification and its purpose is to trap errors in the specification.
- **Research** – This aims to assist in the investigation of a complex or difficult area. It can be done at any time, but gives most benefit after requirements are well understood and before Physical Design.

Documents used in a prototyping exercise are:

- Prototype Pathway;
- Prototype Demonstration Objective Document;
- Prototype Result Log;
- Prototyping Report.

Prototype Pathway This is a schematic showing the components of a user dialogue to be prototyped. It indicates the sequence in which menus and dialogues will be executed. It is used to plan and design the prototype.

Prototype Demonstration Objective Document Its purpose is to ensure that the prototyping demonstration is well-organized and that the maximum benefit is gained from the time spent with the user. It lists the points of discussion to be addressed.

Prototype Result Log This is like the minutes of a meeting. Each change to the prototype requested by the user is logged and graded according to its impact on the Requirements Specification.

Prototyping Report This documents the conclusions of the exercise, covering:

- Was the original prototyping scope covered?
- Were the objectives met?
- What SSADM products have been/should be changed?

• Lessons learned.

Prototyping Activities The following activities describe the production of a prototype:

• Obtain style guide;
• Define the prototype scope;
• Prototype initial menu structures;
• Develop prototype combinations of menus and screens;
• Prepare for the prototype demonstration;
• Demonstrate and review prototype;
• Make changes to SSADM documentation and produce report.

Dialogue Design

Purpose Dialogues define all the on-line interactions with users. Dialogue Identi-fication and Design define the requirements for dialogue based on the functions of the system. In close consultation with the users, the dialogues are specified in terms of the data being passed between system and user. The navigation structure within which dialogues are accessed is designed with reference to:

• the user's job;
• the type of technology which will be used to implement the dialogues;
• the user's skill and knowledge.

This concentrates on the user's direct interaction with the system and is therefore of utmost importance in the analysis and design of a quality system.

Dialogue Design is used to capture and represent the on-line activities of a system on two levels:

• The logical definition of exchanges between the user and functions in terms of data items and messages.
• The mapping of the dialogues to the target technology of the new system, for example Graphical User Interface or character-based technology.

Although the second level may be seen as a Physical Design issue, it is an area that can greatly influence the specification of dialogues much earlier than Physical Design.

Overview Within the System Development Template dialogues are an essential element of External Design in the area of Specification. Dialogue Design requires substantial knowledge of the User Organization to build the User Catalogue and identify user roles.

Identification and design of the dialogues is independent of the processing requirements for the system. This is achieved by specifying dialogues based upon functions and user rather than upon events/enquiries although these events and

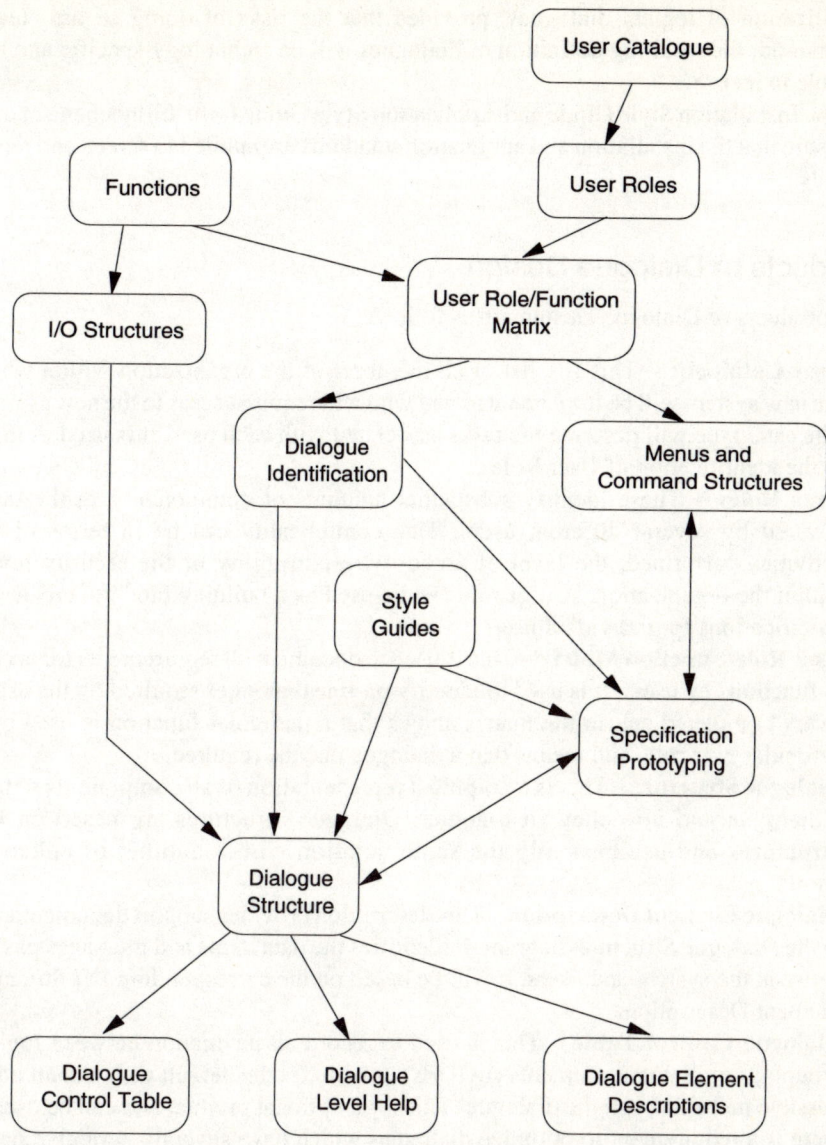

Figure 5.10 Dialogue Design components

enquiries will ultimately be invoked via the dialogue itself. Thus the 'system' view is represented by the events linked to the functions while the 'user' view is represented by the dialogues.

Dialogues may be developed using prototyping tools to implement the dialogues directly in the target environment. In this case projects may not need to complete the specification of logical dialogues, provided that the risks of doing so are clearly understood; the resulting definition of dialogues will be technology-specific and less flexible in its use.

The Installation Style Guide and Application Style Guide form the mechanism used to ensure that the installation and application standards are applied to screen and report layouts.

Products of Dialogue Design

The products of Dialogue Design are as follows:

- **User Catalogue** – This is a list of all members of the organization within which the new system will be implemented and who will require access to the new system. The catalogue will describe the tasks associated with each user. It is used as input to the identification of User Roles.
- **User Roles** – These identify substantial amounts of commonality in the tasks covered by several different users. This commonality can be in terms of the activities performed, the level of authority/responsibility or the security levels within the organization. A user role can be used as a building block to create job specifications for individual users.
- **User Role/Function Matrix** – This is used to document all requirements for access to functions by users. It is used to identify on-line dialogues required by the users. Every completed cell in the matrix shows that a particular function is used by a particular user role, and means that a dialogue may be required.
- **Dialogue Structure** – This is a graphical representation of all components within a dialogue and how they fit together. Dialogue Structures are based on I/O Structures and use basically the same notation with a number of enhancements.
- **Dialogue Element Description** – This description provides support documentation to the Dialogue Structure diagram. It identifies the data items and messages passed between the system and users. It will be based on the corresponding I/O Structure Element Description.
- **Dialogue Control Table** – This is used to record all navigation between logical groupings of dialogue elements (LGDEs). It includes the default path and all other possible paths through the dialogue. This is an optional product and can be used if there is a requirement to optimize dialogues which have several alternative paths or to size the on-line system.
- **Dialogue Level Help** – This document lists any dialogue level help identified. It is an optional product.
- **Menu and Command Structures** – Menu Structures are a graphical representation of the way menus and dialogues are organized for each User Role. Command Structures link dialogues that support a coherent task in the user's job specification, creating the effect of a continuous dialogue without returning to menus. Each user role will be associated with a single Menu Structure. Command Structures are defined as options for direct navigation from a single dialogue.

Physical Design

Introduction The purpose of Physical Design is to specify the physical data, processes, inputs and outputs using the language and features of the chosen physical environment and incorporating installation standards. The integrity of the Logical Design is maintained as far as possible, while exploiting the strengths of the implementation products and minimizing their weaknesses. Essential performance requirements are also addressed.

The basic process of Physical Design is:

- Prepare for Physical Design:
  - Learn the rules of the implementation environment.
  - Review the precise requirements for logical to physical mapping.
  - Plan the approach.
- Complete the specification of functions.
- Incrementally and iteratively develop the data and process designs using a cycle of:
  - design;
  - test against objectives;
  - optimize;
  - review.

Prepare for Physical Design This involves learning about the target hardware and software, and planning the way forward for Physical Design. It includes collection of all the required documents.

The SSADM products which are used in Physical Process Specification are:

- the Requirements Catalogue ;
- the Technical System Architecture developed to describe the selected Technical System Option;
- Conceptual Process Modelling products (Enquiry Access Paths and Effect Correspondence Diagrams, or Enquiry Process Models and Update Process Models);
- Dialogue Structures with Menu Structures and Command Structures;
- Function Definitions;
- Required System Logical Data Model and Data Catalogue.

In addition, the following products should be obtained from local policies and procedures (or developed if they are not available):
- Processing System Classification (this will identify the features of the implementation technology which can be used to implement features of the SSADM technology – types of tools available, mix of procedural and non-procedural languages, database processing and dialogue features).
- Application Development Standards including:
  - Application Style Guide;
  - Application Naming Standards;
  - Physical Design Strategy.

Preparation for Physical Design can be initiated as soon as the implementation environment and technology have been determined. Both preparation and implementation will vary from project to project depending upon:

- procurement issues;
- local standards and technical policies of the organization;
- the existence of other parallel and related projects;
- the timing of Technical System Options.

Physical Design Strategy　Physical Design includes the definition of a strategy for implementing the Logical Design in a specific environment, stating how best to use the facilities provided by that environment. The Physical Design Strategy is based on a general classification scheme which identifies the major data handling, performance and processing characteristics of the target environment. The explanation of how to use the features of a specific product may be provided (in full or in part) by the product supplier in an 'interface guide'. With or without this guide, it is imperative that the Physical Design team have or develop expertise in the use of the specific implementation products.

Physical Process Specification　The Logical Design is usually not at a sufficient level of completeness or detail for direct implementation in a physical environment. For example, it does not contain full details of the processing associated with the reporting and correcting of syntax errors.

In Physical Design, after completing the Logical Design, the designer carries out program specification and design, based on the Function Component Implementation Map (FCIM), which specifies the packaging of processing components into units for implementation and the relationships between these units, including re-use. Activities include:

- physical specification of the External Design, including dialogues, batch input–output programs, transient files;
- physical specification of the Conceptual Model, including update and enquiry processes and (if applicable) automated business activities;
- the Process Data Interface (PDI), which hides the physical database design from the Conceptual Model, and allows update and enquiry processes to be written as if they accessed the Logical Data Model.

Physical Data Design　The scope of the term Physical Data Design is very broad. In SSADM the term refers specifically to the study of the complex issues of:

- physical data placement;
- DBMS optimization.

SSADM provides general rules of thumb applicable to most DBMSs or file handlers for quickly producing an initial physical data model. Product specific rules can then be applied. Timing and sizing is carried out on the design and, if necessary, changes are made to the design to meet performance and space objectives.

Physical Data Design

Purpose   The objective of Physical Data Design is to develop a design which:

- implements the new system's data requirements as defined in the Required System Logical Data Model;
- supports the system's processing requirements;
- meets the space and timing objectives set for the system.

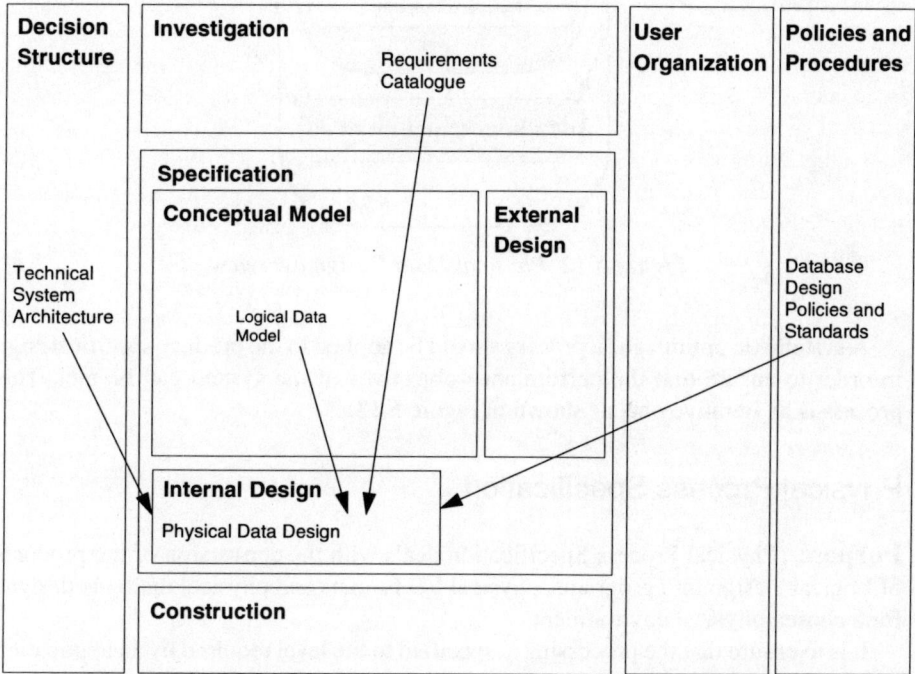

Figure 5.11 Physical Data Design in the System Development Template

Overview   Physical Data Design is in the Internal Design area of the System Development Template. A Required System Logical Data Model is an implementation-independent design. When an implementation environment has been selected, the Required System Logical Data Model must be transformed into a database or file design which is expressed in terms of the physical storage and access facilities provided in that implementation environment. Figure 5.12 gives an overview of Physical Data Design as described in this chapter.

The product-specific Physical Data Design cannot be guaranteed to meet the performance objectives for the system, even though that design has been pre-optimized by application of heuristics (rules of thumb), such as the least dependent occurrence rule (when it is possible to store an entity in two or more physical hierarchies, it should be stored in the one in which it occurs least).

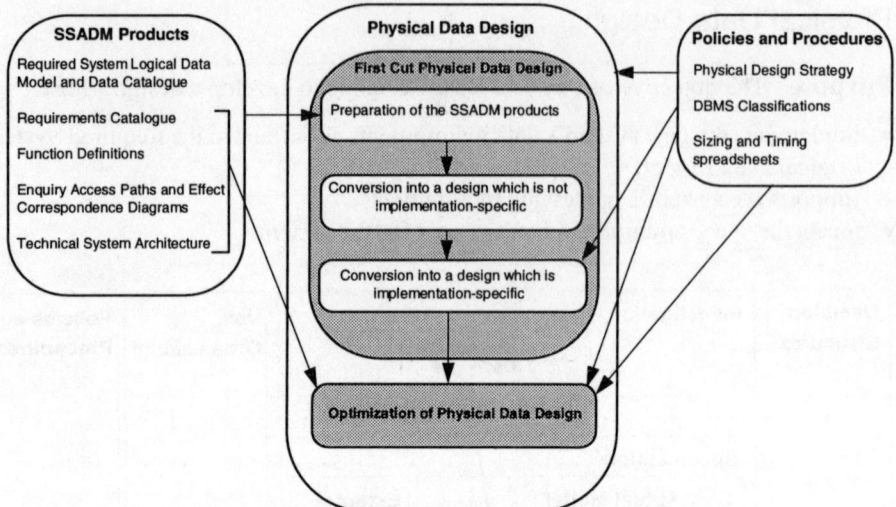

Figure 5.12 Physical Data Design overview

A systematic optimization process should be applied to the product-specific design in order to ensure that the performance objectives of the system can be met. This process is an iterative one, as shown in Figure 5.13.

Physical Process Specification

Purpose   Physical Process Specification deals with the conversion of the products of Logical Design into programs, physical I/O formats and physical dialogue designs for a chosen physical environment.

It is to ensure that the processing is specified to the level required by an application generator or a programmer to develop programs.

Overview   The technique guides designers in the approach to taking a Logical Design and specifying a system's physical processes, taking into account information about the selected physical processing system with which they are working. Much of the technique is specific to the target environment.

The approach to Physical Process Specification is based upon the 3-schema Specification Architecture. The separation of concerns between the Conceptual Model, External Design and Internal Design should be preserved into Physical Design.

This separation of concerns in Physical Design has several advantages:

- The transition from logical to physical is made easier.
- The logical products from SSADM can be mapped more readily on to elements of the Physical Design which will assist in maintenance and future development.
- Physical design requirements are addressed in three smaller areas rather than in one large one.

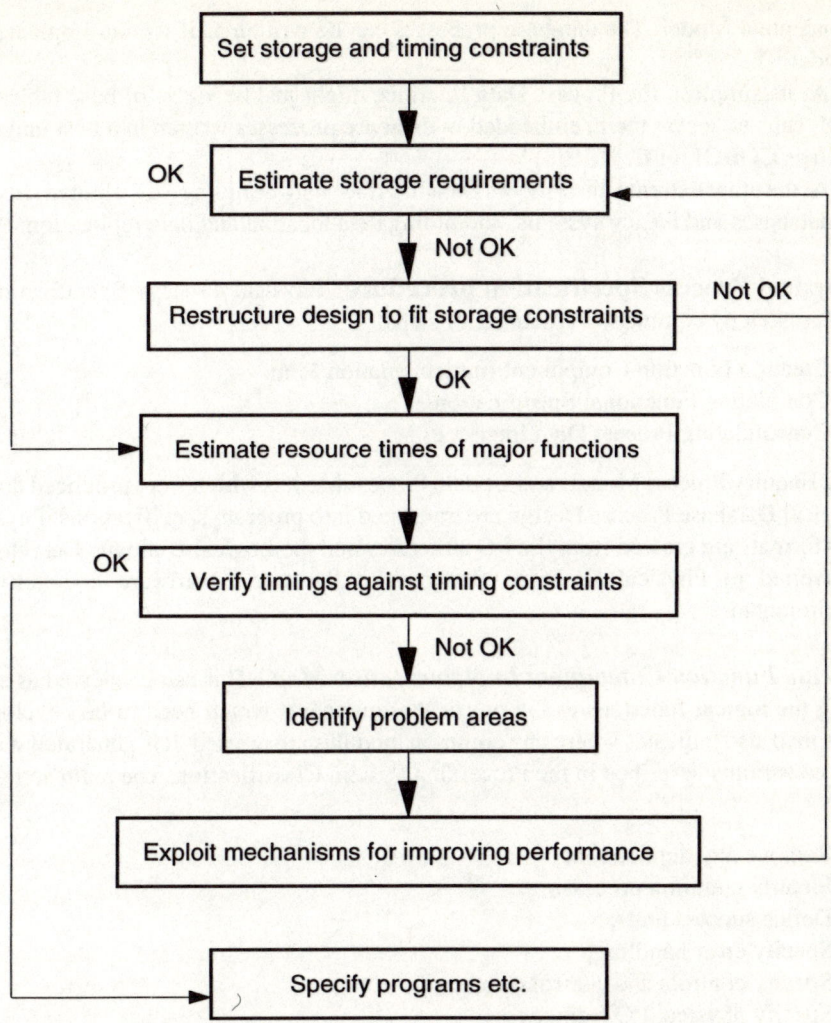

Figure 5.13 Physical Data Design Optimization

- The Physical Process Specification will map more readily on to a variety of architectures including client/server and distributed systems. Different technologies may be used for the three schemata, with well-defined interfaces between them. For example, the External Design may be delivered on multiple platforms and the Internal Design may be implemented on a mix of DBMSs.
- Access to legacy system data (and other shared databases) can be hidden behind a Process Data Interface (PDI).

Process Data Interface The Process Data Interface is a layer of software which 'hides' the physical database from the database update and enquiry processes in the

Conceptual Model. The database processes can be written as if for the Logical Data Model.

At its simplest, the Process Data Interface might just be views of base tables and SQL calls to access them, embedded in database processes written in a host language such as COBOL or C.

At the other extreme, the Process Data Interface may be hiding a distributed network of databases and legacy systems, and hiding data location and data replication.

Physical Process Specification procedure Physical Process Specification is undertaken by completing a number of steps:

- Creating Function Component Implementation Map.
- Completing Functional Specification.
- Consolidating Process Data Interface.

The Enquiry Process Models and Update Process Models which were produced during Logical Database Process Design are translated into program specifications. Physical I/O formats are created from the I/O structures and the Logical Dialogue Designs are converted to Physical Dialogue Designs for the target hardware and software environment.

Create Function Component Implementation Map This can be viewed as mapping the logical functions to the physical components which need to be developed. The map also indicates where any common modules are re-used. It is generated within the constraints described in the Processing System Classification. The main activities are:

- Remove any duplication;
- Identify common processing;
- Define success units;
- Specify error handling;
- Specify controls and control errors;
- Specify physical I/O formats;
- Specify physical dialogues.

Complete Function Specification There are two areas of requirement for completion of the processing specification:

- External Design;
- Conceptual Model.

External Design. The bridging between dialogue and database processes will, in the majority of cases, be a relatively straightforward process. A dialogue will often require a single screen which represents a single event or enquiry. It is unlikely that any further specification will be needed for this type of function. However, it is possible that the data input and output through the dialogue do not exactly match the event and enquiry data specified in Effect Correspondence Diagrams and Enquiry Access Paths. In this case, some form of transformation process will be required. This transformation may involve:

- decomposing input data into multiple event/enquiry triggers, possibly including selections and iterations of events and enquiries;
- reference data look-ups (pre-event enquiries that are not made visible to the dialogue) and local calculation.

The function may have to consolidate event and enquiry response data for presentation in the dialogue. This may involve:

- collating responses from several events/enquiries;
- sorting, suppressing duplicates;
- calculation of summary data.

Conceptual Model. The additional specification for the Conceptual Model may be in the automation of business activities. Each business activity that is to be automated will contain rules that have to be expressed in a form that can be implemented. Some conceptual processes may have to be restructured to obtain performance from the database (typical cases include doing batch updates in two passes with the input sorted in different sequences, or postponing full updates for transactions input during peak hours).

Consolidate Process Data Interface   The Process Data Interface (PDI) converts accesses to the Logical Data Model into accesses to the Physical Data Design. It is the interface between the Physical Data Design and the Physical Process Specification. It allows the designer to implement the logical update and enquiry processes as physical programs, independently of the physical database structure.

Where the physical data model does not match the logical model, the PDI is needed to bridge the gap between logical accesses in the application processes and the physical data these are trying to reach. The differences between logical and physical data may arise because of constraints in the way the data is held – DBMS limitations, performance or storage considerations – or because the system must be implemented on an existing database.

The main benefit of a PDI to the designer is that application processing is separated from the data on which it operates. A database may be amended without reorganizing the system – or vice versa. In either case the PDI is modified to reflect the changes, a simple operation compared to changing either of the other two.

The access requirements documented in the Function Component Implementation Map are matched against the Physical Data Design and any mismatches noted. Then a sequence of physical accesses is determined which will meet the logical view of the FCIM.

6
Policies and Procedures

Style Guides

Purpose A Style Guide is a set of standards for the human–computer interface (HCI). It should be used when designing dialogues, screens and reports. Its purpose is to ensure:

- consistency in data presentation and user interaction with an application;
- consistency across systems;
- standard notification and handling of errors;
- consistent use of function keys, other special keys or key combinations and the mouse.

Overview The use of style guides ensures a common look and feel across all facilities within the application. This can help users to become familiar with new applications rapidly if the interface works the same way in all contexts. If the same style guide is adopted across all applications, the training required in the use of new applications will be greatly reduced for those users already familiar with existing ones.

The use of a style guide can accelerate a project for two reasons:

- The effort required in designing the user interface is reduced.
- Commercially available style guides sometimes contain component libraries which can be used to assemble a working user interface.

SSADM refers to:

- an Installation Style Guide which sets broad standards for all applications within the organization as a whole;
- the Application Style Guide which is an elaboration of the Installation Style Guide for use on a particular project.

Ideally, the Installation Style Guide should be put in place before any project is initiated. In practice, it is often developed in parallel with the first application and then adopted by subsequent projects.

Where specific user interface standards are to be used to develop a system, it is possible to purchase off-the-shelf style guides such as the Microsoft Windows Style

Guide and OSF Motif Guide. Further help is given in *SSADM and GUI Design: a Project Manager's Guide* in the System Development Library.

All dialogue design, prototyping, screen and report design should be done with reference to the style guide. Here are some examples of the typical areas covered by a style guide.

User interface style
menus
forms
graphical interfaces

User guidance
layout
colour
sentence content
help
layout
content
access prompts

System response times
perception of delay
warning messages
delay time recommendations

Tailoring the user interface
adaptability to the task
environment
adaptability to the individual preference

Using colour displays
general guidelines
how many colours?
which colours?

Calendar
date display
time display

'Welcome' displays
basic requirements
identifying the system
log-on procedures
copyright information
exit from the screen

Keyboard and mouse
key assignment

use of pointing device
number of buttons/keys
major/minor buttons

Menus
basic menu requirements
when to use menus
categorizing menus
rules for subdividing menus
menu titles
menu option short cuts
temporarily unavailable options
selected option
accessing the menus
transient menu item selection
immediate selection and invocation

Dialogue boxes
selection of multiple items within dialogue boxes
OK screen button
Cancel screen button

Forms and dialogue boxes
scope
movement within forms
field validation
error messages and help information
completing the form

Report Issues
display of time and date
line length
layout of fields
standard footers
end of report page
font size
page depth
standard headers
beginning of report page
amount of information on page

Part III
CUSTOMIZATION

7

Customizing SSADM4+

Customizing SSADM can either start from the default Structural Model as described here, or can start from many other points. These are identified in the publication *Customizing SSADM*. Help is also given on alternative customization starting points in other publications. In the bibliography at the back of this book a list is provided of the publications available in the System Development Library which describe customization processes in greater detail. SSADM does not try to cover the entire life cycle of a system. It is a generic method which can be used from a feasibility study up to the point at which a specific hardware and/or software environment must be chosen. It provides a complete application development framework and the associated procedures for capturing and analysing requirements and specifying a system design.

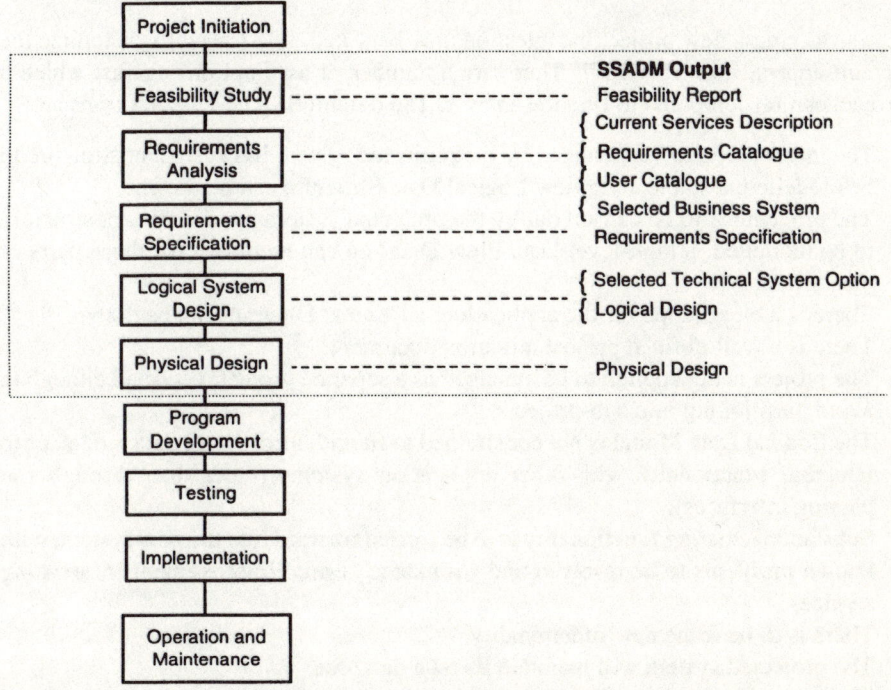

Figure 7.1 Overview of SSADM's Default Structural Model

71

This framework offers a flexible, customizable method which enables its use within a properly planned, managed and controlled project.

In SSADM the model above is called the default Structural Model. It shows a typical linear progression through an IS development. Today there are other methods of development, such as RAD, where there are opportunities for some of the modules to be iterated and/or developed in parallel. Whatever the method, it will be reflecting some part of this default model and all methods will get management benefits from the SSADM framework.

A Structural Model is a kind of road map for a project. It breaks the activities involved in a development project into smaller, more manageable chunks of work. A Structural Model is subdivided into modules, stages within modules and then steps within stages. Each step describes:

- inputs;
- outputs;
- techniques to be used in developing products;
- activities in which the techniques are used.

The products developed in each step build up into packages delivered at the end of stages on which project decisions are based.

Default Project Assumptions

In considering a new project the question may be asked, 'Do I need to customize the default approach to SSADM?' There are a number of assumptions against which a project can be compared to find the answer. The default SSADM assumptions are:

- The information to be managed by the projected system has sufficient structure to be modelled: a stable, overview Logical Data Structure can be drawn.
- The procedures to be carried out by the projected system have sufficient structure to be modelled: a high-level Data Flow Diagram can be drawn for those parts of the system.
- There is a clear scope for the application: a Context Diagram can be drawn.
- There is a well-defined project initiation document.
- The project is big enough to be managed as a separate project, yet small enough to avoid partitioning into sub-projects.
- The Logical Data Model is not constrained to fit with a corporate data model, or to integrate functionally with other application systems (other than through file passing interfaces).
- Substantial existing functionality is to be carried forward into the new system, with known problems to be resolved and with some desired improvements of existing services.
- There is to be some new functionality.
- The projected system will maintain its own database.
- There is sufficient freedom in information systems strategy, corporate policies and

organizational procedures, together with a range of non-mandatory requirements, to consider a range of business options.

- There is sufficient freedom in procurement policy and technical standards to consider a range of technical options.
- The project will use the 'waterfall' life cycle model which is based on the notion that there is a single delivery date for the complete system and that a development project is represented by a smooth progression of successive stages with minimal iteration. In SSADM this model is assumed, all planning is towards a single delivery date and all analysis and design is done in detail before coding and testing.
- There are sufficient project resources, particularly in the technical areas of analysis and design, to follow the default method specification.

Nevertheless, each project is different. There is no single project structure which suits all projects. How does SSADM approach this difficulty? It offers the default Structural Model as a *basis* for deciding what structure is right for each project. It is not expected that any project will ever use the default structure unchanged. SSADM *expects* it to be customized.

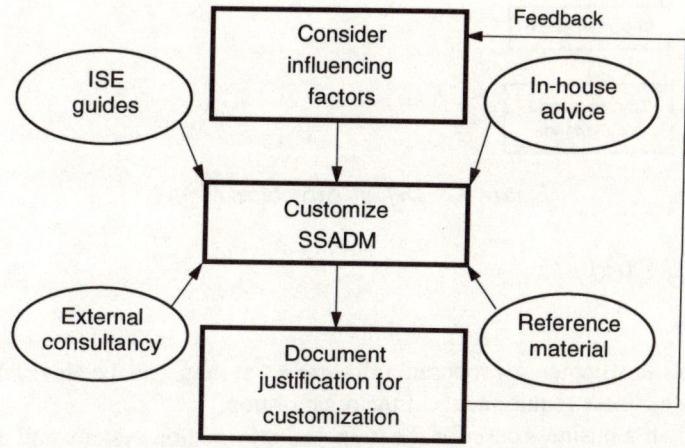

Figure 7.2 The customizing process

The default Structural Model is based on a set of underlying assumptions about project objectives, type of application and target implementation environment. SSADM will need to be customized either because some of these assumptions do not apply, or to adjust the method to the specific detail of the project. For example, a standard product may be needed, but not in the full detail specified in the Reference Manual.

This section of the book starts with a brief description of the default Structural Model only to offer the reader one start point. Then an example of customizing SSADM is discussed to give an idea of the customization process.

The Default Structural Model

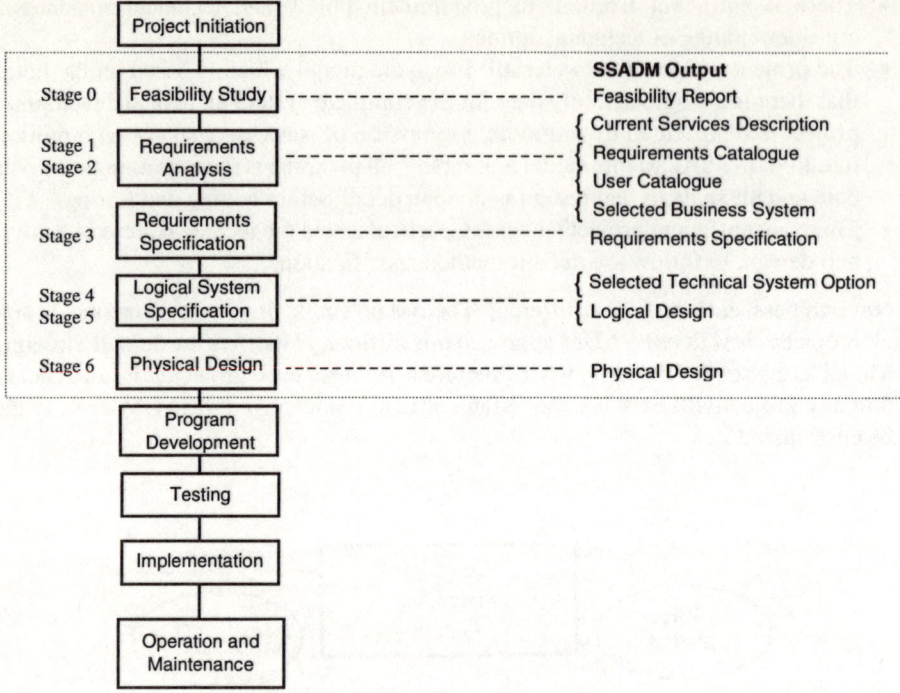

Figure 7.3 Default Structural Model

Feasibility Study

Objectives

- To establish whether a proposed information system can be devised to meet specified business requirements of the organization.
- To establish a business case for the proposed information system, and enable the Project Board to decide whether to commit resources to a more detailed study.
- To determine whether to proceed in a different direction from that envisaged in the IS Strategy.
- To enable the Project Board to select from a range of business and technical options, and to identify the project(s) necessary to implement the chosen option.
- To investigate to a level only where a realistic decision can be made on the direction and resources of the project.

Requirements Analysis

In SSADM Requirements Analysis is driven by the Investigation of the Current Environment and Business System Options. The emphasis then moves to the future system. Requirements are documented in the Requirements Catalogue expressed in terms of system objectives. These are related to levels of service, security considerations and overall functionality. Each is expressed in as quantifiable a way as possible. This greatly helps the user organization verify the acceptability of all products developed by the team.

The Requirements Catalogue is supported by Data Flow Models of current functionality, and a Logical Data Model of the information used in current services.

Business System Options are presented for management to choose the scope of the required system functionality and to commit to its planned costs.

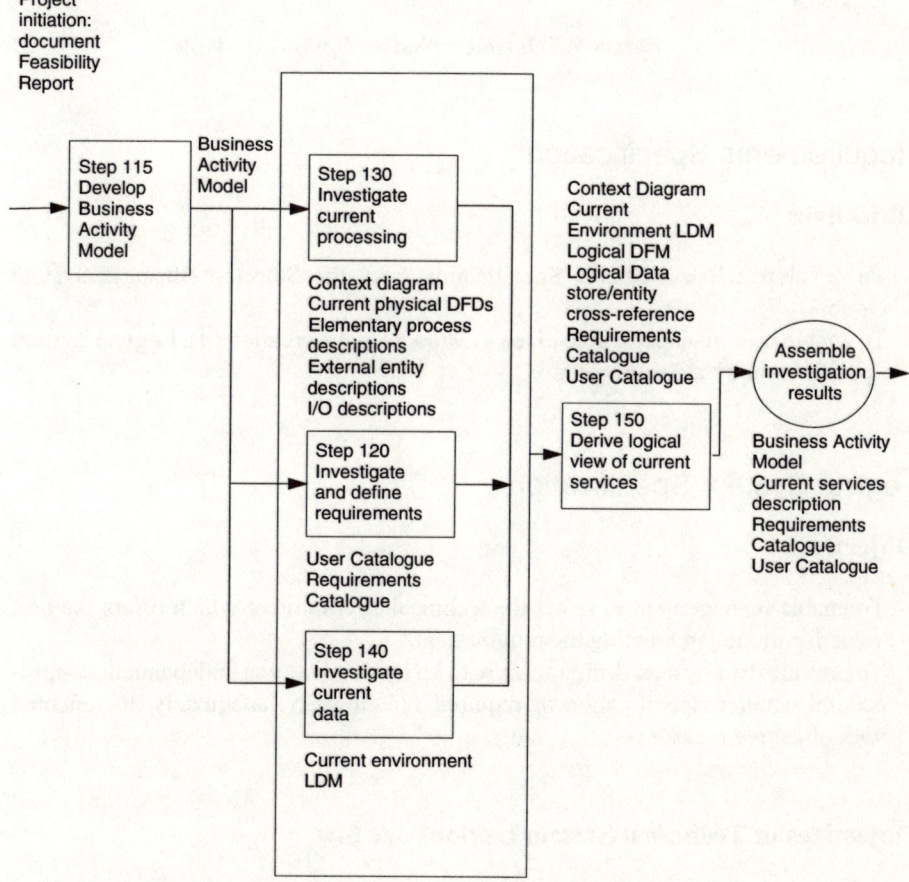

Figure 7.4 Investigation of Current Environment

Objectives of Business System Options are to:

- Define a range of business solutions.
- Create a short-list of options.
- Have a business solution selected by the Project Board.
- Agree the project scope and any interfaces.

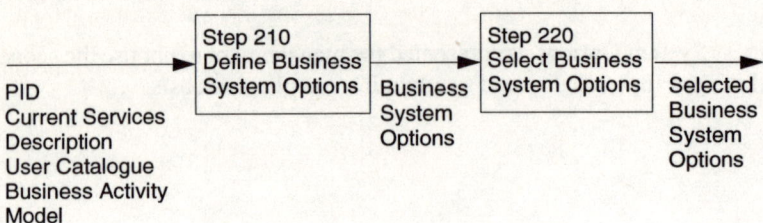

PID
Current Services
Description
User Catalogue
Business Activity
Model

Figure 7.5 Business System Options

Requirements Specification

Objectives

- To develop a Requirements Specification from the Selected Business System Option.
- To enable user management to place a contract for the creation of a Logical System Specification by a design team.

Logical System Specification

Objectives

- To enable management to select the technical environment which offers the best value for money in meeting the requirement.
- To provide the physical design team with an implementation-independent nonprocedural detailed specification of required functionality, adequately documented with objective measures.

Objectives of Technical System Options are to:

- To identify and define different ways of implementing physically the Requirements Specification.
- To make a decision on the option to go forward to the next stage as the hardware and software basis of the Physical System Design.

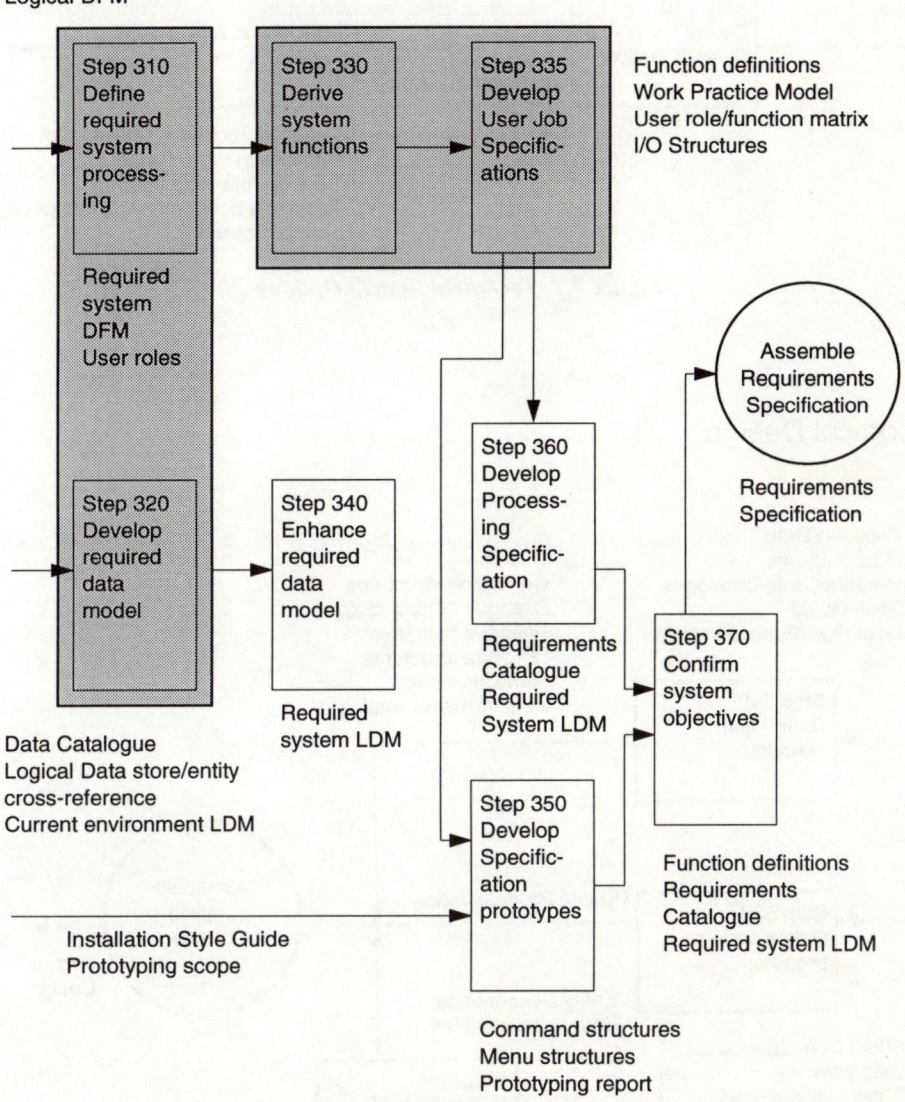

Figure 7.6 Requirements Specification

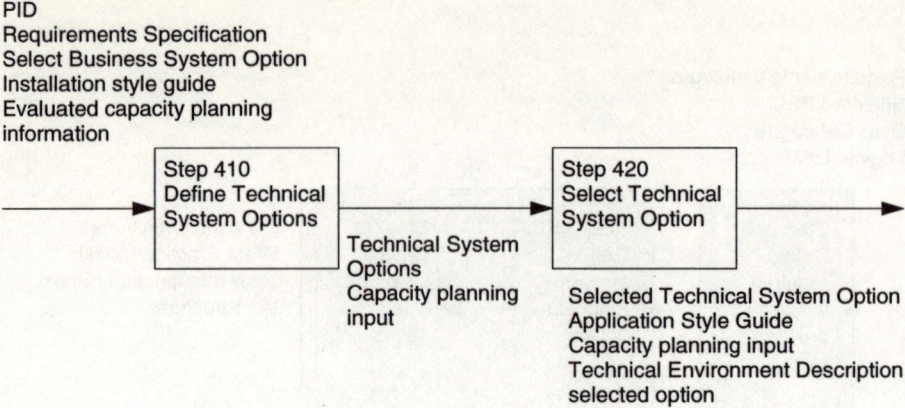

PID
Requirements Specification
Select Business System Option
Installation style guide
Evaluated capacity planning
information

Step 410
Define Technical
System Options

Technical System
Options
Capacity planning
input

Step 420
Select Technical
System Option

Selected Technical System Option
Application Style Guide
Capacity planning input
Technical Environment Description
selected option

Figure 7.7 Technical System Options

Logical Design

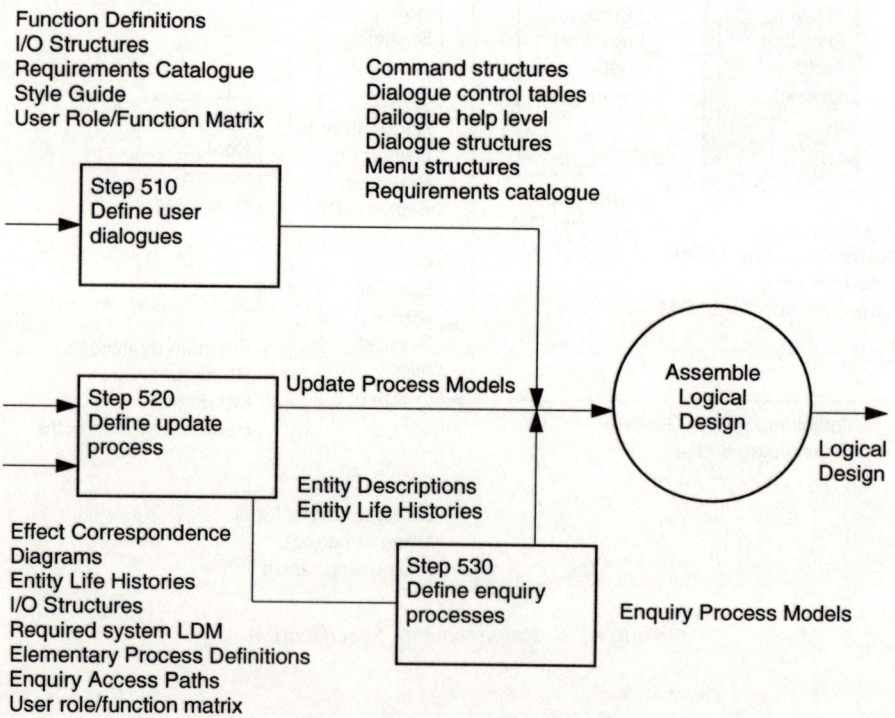

Function Definitions
I/O Structures
Requirements Catalogue
Style Guide
User Role/Function Matrix

Command structures
Dialogue control tables
Dailogue help level
Dialogue structures
Menu structures
Requirements catalogue

Step 510
Define user
dialogues

Step 520
Define update
process

Update Process Models

Assemble
Logical
Design

Logical
Design

Entity Descriptions
Entity Life Histories

Effect Correspondence
Diagrams
Entity Life Histories
I/O Structures
Required system LDM
Elementary Process Definitions
Enquiry Access Paths
User role/function matrix

Step 530
Define enquiry
processes

Enquiry Process Models

Figure 7.8 Logical Design

Objectives of Logical Design are to:

- To create a detailed Logical Design of the required system from the Requirements Specification.
- To provide the basis for Physical Design.
- To provide a detailed specification which:
  - is nonprocedural;
  - can be implemented in a range of technical environments;
  - maximizes opportunities for re-use;
  - can absorb any business changes prior to physical implementation.

Physical Design

Objectives

- To specify the physical data, processes, inputs and outputs, using the language and features of the chosen physical environment and incorporating installation standards.

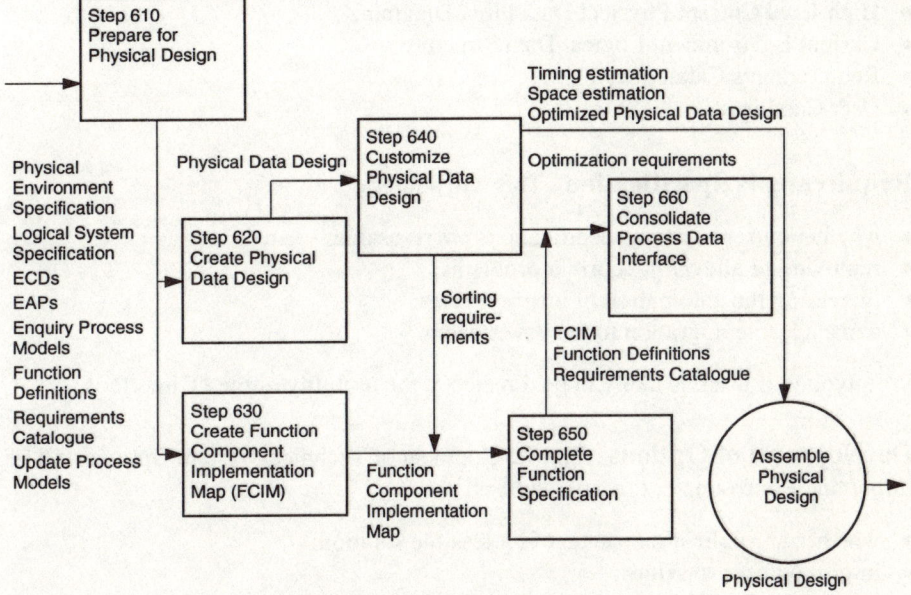

Figure 7.9 Physical Design

Example of SSADM Customization

Customizing SSADM for different types of Feasibility Study

Whatever its purpose, a Feasibility Study is a microcosm of:

- Investigation;

- Requirements Specification;
- Development of options.

Two typical variants of a Feasibility Study are:

- replacement of an IT system;
- evolution of business activity.

The SSADM techniques required differ in each of these variants.

Replacement of an IT system

The reason for this type of Feasibility Study might be obsolete equipment, the termination of a rental agreement or difficulty in maintaining the current application software.

Investigation   Major SSADM products will be:

- High-level Current Physical Data Flow Diagram;
- Current Environment Logical Data Structure;
- Requirements Catalogue;
- User Catalogue.

Requirements Specification   This will address:

- whether current system specifications are re-usable;
- removing or alleviating current problems;
- increasing the automation of business rules;
- a manageable migration to the new system.

Prototyping, if used, is likely to be directed at the usability of the IT interface.

Development of Options   The development of Technical System Options will be important. For example, this will address:

- whether an application package is a feasible solution;
- impact on user activities;
- the possibility of integrating currently separate services.

Evolution of business activity

Here the business activity has changed since the current information system was developed and an upgrade is needed.

Investigation   Major SSADM products will be the same as in the example for the replacement of an IT system with the addition of a Business Activity Model.

Requirements Definition Again this is similar to the previous example, but emphasis here would be on the information support requirements of the Business Activity Model rather than the current IT system. Based on this the approach would be to consider:

- what current services can be carried forward;
- what new services are required.

Development of options Options will be concerned with:

- whether the current system should be adapted or replaced;
- which of the new or changed business activities can be automated;
- the impact on the user.

SSADM Customization for a Full Study

Another common application of SSADM is for a Full Study where a new business area requires support from an information system. There is no existing system, either automated or manual, to enhance or replace.

SSADM product modifications The Investigation area of the System Development Template will undergo radical change. The impact is illustrated in figure 7.10.

Since there is no current system, it will be impossible to build a Current Services Description. Consequently, the requirements analysis and specification must be driven solely by the projected requirements of the new system. Hence special emphasis must be given to the preparation of the Requirements Catalogue.

Although there is no current system to analyse, the new system may need to interact with external systems. As a result the interfaces with any external systems must be analysed.

The Context Diagram will be based on the required system and will be an important aid in assessing what the new system is to achieve.

An initial Logical Data Structure will be developed, also based on the required system. It will only comprise the principal data entities. It will not be a formal deliverable, but will provide assistance in the development of Business System Options.

The User Catalogue will be based on the new business organization, which may still be changing. If the new organization has not been finalized during Stage 1 this product may yield little benefit and could be omitted.

The emphasis in the Business System Options will be on the organization and structure of the business which requires the new system. Multiple versions of the Logical Data Structure and Data Flow Model may be constructed to support various business options. However, both of these products will be kept to a high level at this point (Stage 2).

The development of the full Required System Data Flow Model and Logical Data Model in Stage 3 will require additional effort. They will be derived from the

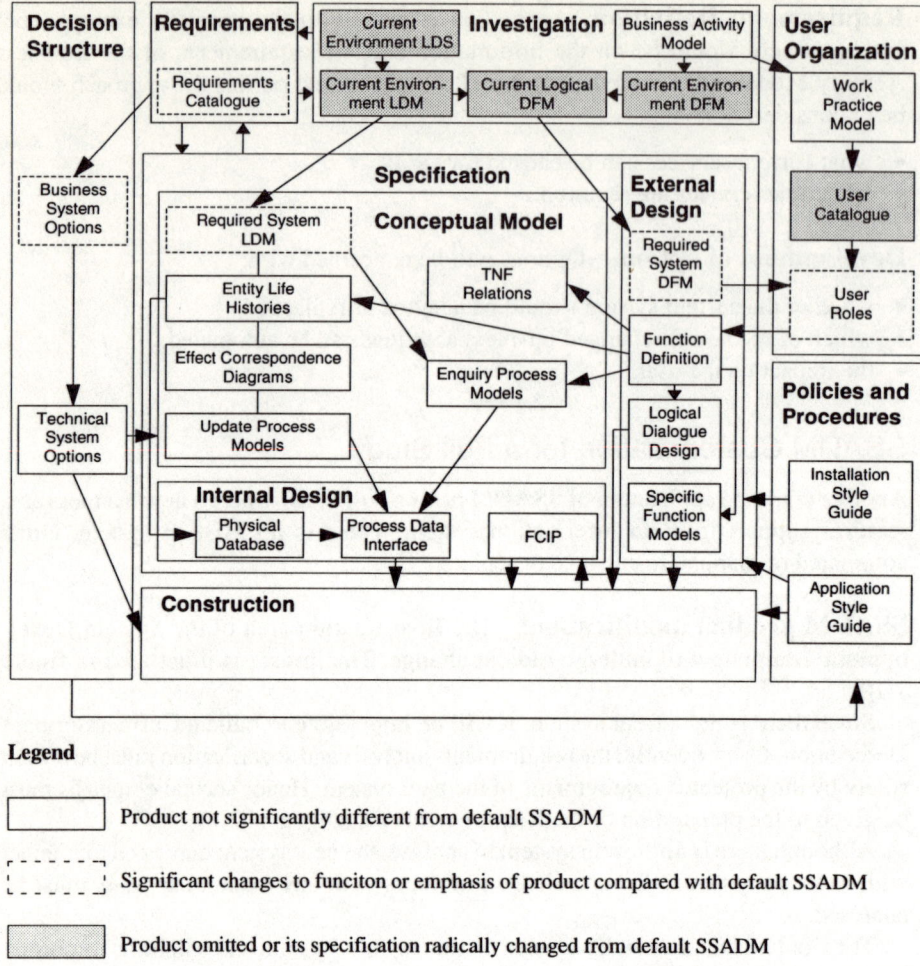

Legend

☐   Product not significantly different from default SSADM

⌐‐‐‐‐‐¬   Significant changes to funciton or emphasis of product compared with default SSADM

▓   Product omitted or its specification radically changed from default SSADM

Figure 7.10 Product modifications for new business area project

higher-level products in Stage 2 and cannot derive information from a Current System Data Flow Model and Logical Data Model.

Extra emphasis will be required on the business system development, since there is no current system on which to base the new organization. In particular, special consideration will be required in the definition of User Roles. There is also likely to be increased uncertainty about how the new system will be operated. Hence specification prototyping could be of benefit.

Default Structural Model changes

- Stage 1 – Special emphasis on Step 120, since Steps 130 to 150 will be omitted. However, the interfaces with external systems must be investigated.

- Stage 2 – Special emphasis on the organization and structure of the business.
- Stage 3 – Extra work in Steps 310 and 320. Special emphasis on business system with probable use of specification prototyping.

An evolutionary development approach could be considered to cater for a new business venture 'settling down' and to allow for the uncertainty which is likely to apply to a new situation's business needs.

Annex: Project Procedures

The project procedures described in this annex are not part of SSADM, but they are an important part of every project. The procedures are described briefly, together with how they interact and interface with SSADM.

Capacity Planning

Purpose

Capacity Planning techniques are used to help organizations predict hardware capacity requirements and decide the right performance/cost balance for their needs. They are also used to influence the design of systems to optimize their performance and that of other systems sharing the same hardware.

Overview

Concepts used in Capacity Planning are:

- **Service Level Requirements** (SLRs) – These describe how the users require each on-line transaction or batch job to perform. They include response or turn-round times, throughput or concurrence. The operating efficiency of the proposed configuration is specified in terms of SLRs. Resilience, availability, contingency and security are examples of system-wide SLRs.
- **Service Level Agreements** (SLAs) – These are negotiated between the users and IT service providers when the system has been implemented and accepted by both parties as satisfactory. An SLA will detail the mutually agreed levels of each SLR.

If the new application is to be implemented on existing equipment, Capacity Planning will be able to assess whether the service level requirements for the new application can be met without significant impact on the existing Service Level Agreements and also to assess whether the hardware requires upgrading.

Capacity Planning and SSADM

The Requirements Catalogue contains the target performance level for each function. The required data storage capacity for the new system can be calculated by aggregating the size and number of occurrences of each entity. Some idea of the relative importance of different data stores is needed so that estimates can be made about data distribution and the number of disks drives which will be required.

Each Technical System Option will be supported by a Technical System Architecture. This can be used to provide capacity planning tools with the basis of hardware configurations. Capacity planning will assist in the choice of possible configurations. Capacity Planning assists in testing the design against the requirements and proposed configurations. This enables the system design to be tuned in the light of anticipated results.

Configuration Management

Configuration Management (CM) provides procedures for controlling the products of a project throughout their creation and maintenance and for providing management with information about the status of the products. Configuration Management is defined in the CCTA's IT Infrastructure Library as a discipline, normally supported by software tools, which gives precise control over IT assets by allowing IT management to:

- specify the versions of configuration items in use and in existence in a project, and to give information on:
  - the status of these items (e.g. in live use, archived, under development);
  - who 'owns' each item (the individual with prime responsibility for it);
  - the relationship between items;
- maintain up-to-date records about project products;
- control changes to products by ensuring appropriate authority has been given.

A Configuration Item is any product or component of an IT infrastructure, or an item, such as a request for change, which is under the control of Configuration Management. A Configuration Item may vary widely in complexity, size and type – from an entire system (including all hardware, software and documentation) to a single module. For example, if we consider a car, there would be one Configuration Item record for the complete car, and other records for each assembly, sub-assembly and component. In an IT system there would be a Configuration Item record for the complete system, and one for each item, and level of the Product Breakdown Structure.

Configuration control is generally applied to products which are complete rather than products which represent work in progress. The submission of a product for formal quality review is normally the trigger to bring the product under configuration control.

Configuration Management covers:

- **Configuration identification** – This covers the creation of a naming convention which will provide each product with a unique identifier.

- **Configuration control** – There are several parts to this. There are control procedures and protected libraries to allow the products to be submitted to Configuration Control, copies to be released, the product's status to be changed. There are also reports from the configuration about the status of products and an audit of the configuration records against the physical reality of the products, the equivalent of a stock check.
- **Version control** – Once a product has entered Configuration Control and been approved, that version of the product cannot be changed. A new version is created and linked to the reason for change.
- **Baselines** – A baseline is a set of products which are 'frozen' at a particular version. For example, when passing from Logical Design to Physical Design a baseline is taken so that there is a record of what products were passed across and what version of each product was used.
- **Releases** – A release is also a set of products, often those products which constitute a working version of the system. A release will list which products and their version numbers are being handed over. It will also include details such as hardware and software prerequisites, loading instructions, any testing instructions and running instructions
- **Change Control** – There is normally a close link between Change and Configuration Control. An approved change is linked to the relevant products. If the change is to a product which has previously been approved, a copy of the product is released under the next version number and the change made to that, not to the version which has been approved.

Estimating

For effective project management ability to estimate the amount of work, the resources and the timescale needed to meet project objectives is necessary. The subject of estimating for SSADM projects is covered in two System Development Library volumes, one using Function Point Analysis and the other describing the basic principles of estimating (see the bibliography for details).

The use of Function Point Analysis is recommended for SSADM projects because:

- it is a widely used method which is independent of application programming languages;
- it is well-integrated with SSADM and increasingly supported by SSADM CASE tools;
- there are well-established national and pan-national user groups who are constructing databases of past projects to assist estimators;
- an accurate estimate of the size of a system can be constructed well before physical design.

Maintenance

The real questions for maintenance are:

- Which SSADM techniques will be useful in specifying the kinds of change which are likely to occur in maintenance?
- What is the path from specification products to code during maintenance? How much automated support is provided?

Note that some products are derivable. For example:

- an Update Process Model can be derived from an Effect Correspondence Diagram;
- Required System Data Flow Diagrams, for presentation to users, can be constructed from functions.

In general, derivable products do not need to be maintained.
The issues for maintenance are:

- What implemented products will be affected by change?
- From which repository components are they derived?
- What are the best input views for updating the repository components?

Project Risk Assessment and Management

The basic questions of risk assessment and management are:

- What are the risks to the success of the project?
- What factors are causing the risk?
- How likely is each risk to occur?
- How serious would a risk be to the project if it did occur?
- What can be done to avoid a risk?
- What can be done to lessen or remove a risk's impact?
- How much would this cost?
- What decision does management wish to take in view of the risk analysis?
- What activities are to be added to the plan to monitor the state of the risks?
- At what checkpoints will these be reviewed by user management?

An IT project will be influenced by a number of factors, including project objectives, organizational constraints and situational factors. The implementation strategy for a project is to address the influencing factors with the minimum risk. Risks of possible strategies should be carefully weighed against potential benefits and costs. Table A.1 below lists some suggested situational factors.

Table A.1 Suggested situational factors in project planning

Project aspect	Complexity	Uncertainty
Information system	Heterogeneity of actors Size of target domain Size of distribution Complexity of information Complexity of business processes	Attitude of actors Ability of actors Stability of environment Formality of information Formality of business processes Stability of information and business processes Specificity of information and business processes Understandability of existing system Strategic importance Importance of organizational changes Availability, clarity and stability of requirements Quality of existing specifications
Computer System	Complexity of data Complexity of functions Complexity of non-functional requirements Number of replications of computer system Complexity of target technology	Importance of technological changes Novelty of target technology
Project Task	Size of project Complexity of migration	Novelty of information system development Adequacy of schedules Adequacy of budget
Project Structure	Number of sub-contractors Number of interfaces to other projects and systems	Dependency on sub-contractors Dependency on other projects Formality of customer–customer relationship
Project Actors	Number of project actors	Capability of project team
Project Technology	Complexity of development technology	Novelty of development technology Technology availability

Source: Delivery Planning Guide, Euromethod

Quality Control

Product Descriptions

SSADM recommends that Product Descriptions be written for every major product to be developed. The description is written before the task of creating the product is handed out. It contains Quality Criteria: measurements of quality against which the final product will be compared. Not only does this provide a guide to any reviewers of the final product, but it is also a guide for the person who is creating the product.

Quality Review

The purpose of a Quality Review is to identify errors by means of a planned and documented inspection. A Quality Review is a method whereby a product, group of related products or part of a product is checked by one or more persons against an agreed set of quality criteria. The criteria may comprise the Product Description, the relevant site standards and a checklist. The aim of Quality Reviews is to find any errors in products at the earliest possible time and ensure that these are corrected. A Quality Review consists of three phases:

- preparation;
- review;
- follow up.

The formal roles which must be allocated are those of:

- **Chairman** – The chairman ensures that the review process is properly organized in all three of its phases. In particular this role has the responsibility for the smooth, effective running of the review.
- **Presenter** – The presenter is the author of the product to be reviewed, unless some unusual event prevents this. The aims of this role are firstly to ensure that the reviewers have everything they need to prepare adequately for the review (this may include a brief presentation during the preparation period). During the review the presenter answers any questions from the reviewers as they move towards a joint decision on whether a point is an error or not.
- **Reviewer(s)** – Reviewers have the job of inspecting the product during the preparation phase and asking questions during the review in order to find any errors in the product. During follow-up one or more reviewers must also confirm that any remedial work has corrected the errors found and not caused harmful side-effects.

Where there is a large group of people attending a review, it is often helpful for the chairman to appoint a scribe to write down the action points.

An important part of communication and confidence is to involve the user in Quality Reviews. It is important to ensure that the interested parties attend reviews of critical products, rather than that they are merely represented. This should be part of the stage planning. The products to be delivered are discussed with the user representatives who identify those products which should have reviewers from the user community.

Risk Analysis and Security

This covers the topics of the security of data and the analysis of any risks to that data. SSADM provides an interface with techniques for the analysis of security risk. The CCTA Risk Analysis and Management Method (CRAMM) is compatible with SSADM.

CRAMM is a formalized technique with three phases:

- The assessment of the value of an organization's data;
- The identification and categorizing of any threats against it;
- The recommendation of appropriate counter-measures against those threats.

For data assets, the value attributed is according to the potential impact on the organization of disclosure, corruption, unavailability or destruction of that data. Physical assets are valued in terms of replacement cost. The second phase evaluates the vulnerability of the asset to each identified threat. A typical question would be 'Is there a security need above a minimum level of good practice?' Preventative and protective options are then considered. The cost of the options is weighed against the risk and recommendations made for management approval.

SSADM and CRAMM

The aim of providing an interface between SSADM and CRAMM is to help users give timely consideration to the security requirements of systems throughout the project life cycle. The immediate value of this interface lies in the ability to assess risk and consider appropriate security measures earlier in the development process than is often the case. The long-term value lies in the ability to review security consistently throughout the life cycle of the system.

The three main areas where CRAMM interfaces with SSADM are:

- **Investigation** – An important task at this time is to determine how any existing security arrangements impact the proposed system. Here the analyst has the opportunity to make security personnel/services aware of the new system and begin to involve them. Their requirements can then be considered as part of the analysis activity.
- **Decision Structure** – Business System Options will benefit by ensuring that security requirements and standards are incorporated in the options presented to the project board. Technical System Options may be impacted in terms of security demands on:
  - the operating system (access);
  - communications software (terminal and user validation);

- the application software (access);
- operations support (backup and recovery);
- extra hardware to implement counter-measures.
- **Physical Design** – Security requirements lead to security test plans, operating procedures, and additions to the User and Operations Manuals.

Take-On

Take-On is the conversion of data from the current system for use in the new system. Current data may be held manually, on one or more systems or may need collection from scratch. At Technical System Option selection the system data sources are identified. The I/O Descriptions associated with transactions, the Logical Data Model and the Process Descriptions will all provide definitions of data to enable a Take-On system to be designed and implemented.

Areas for consideration include:

- **Validation** – Is there a need to 'clean' old data to remove duplications and errors?
- **Conversion method** – How is the data to be transferred to the new system?
- **Transfer** – What means will be used to physically link the old system's data to the new?
- **Conversion planning** – The Take-On task is often as complex as a small project in its own right. It needs careful planning to ensure a smooth fit with the implementation of the new system.

Testing

Testing is outside the scope of SSADM but SSADM can contribute to the production of test criteria. Software will pass through a number of different types of test.

Unit testing

Function Definitions say what each functional unit is designed to handle and achieve. Test criteria can be built around the user view of the functions. The development of the Function Definitions allows an early start to the planning of unit tests. The Technical Environment Description will enhance them, bearing in mind that they may need revision after selection of the Technical System Option and Physical Design.

Integration testing

The SSADM products which show how dialogues are grouped together are:

- Conceptual Process Model;
- Command Structures;
- Menu Structures.

System testing

System test planning can begin as soon as the Requirements Catalogue and Function Definitions are available. They can be finalized from the Technical System Architecture and Physical Design. The 'external' and 'internal' constraints bounding the Selected Technical System Option can be seen to specify some of the ways in which the system is expected to behave.

Acceptance testing

The users view of their needs to test the system will be drawn from the:

- Requirements Catalogue;
- Selected Business System Option;
- reasons for selection of the Business System Option (and rejection of the others);
- selected Technical System Option;
- reasons for the selection of the Technical System Option (and rejection of the others).

They will be supplemented by more detailed products from the Requirements Specification and Logical System Specification.

Training

Training needs should be taken into consideration at each of the major SSADM decision points:

- Feasibility Study;
- Business System Options;
- Technical System Options.

Training needs must cover the development staff and user community. Training is often a significant cost element and needs careful planning so that it can occur at the right time for the right people. Training should be considered at four levels:

- **User education** – This is intended to change the way users perceive or think about the system.
- **User training** – This is intended to give users specific skills in using the IT system or the information support it provides.
- **Development staff training** – This is the provision of the necessary skill training in the tools used in the development of the system.
- **Maintenance staff training** – This is not only training in the use of the tools, but training in the philosophy, structure, documentation, modification and management of the operational system.

User training may be built into the user manual or the help system, and therefore becomes a significant amount of work in Physical Design. The User Catalogue is useful in identifying the different classes of user which may need different levels of training. The Technical System Option will show the best type of training. Hands-on training for on-line services may need its own database and terminals. Extra training may be required for the staff doing the conversion work.

Bibliography

The publications are available from:
HMSO Publications Centre, PO Box 276, London SW8 5DT

Accelerated SSADM	ISBN 0 11 330626 1
An Introduction to Reuse	ISBN 0 11 330625 3
Application Partitioning and Integration with SSADM	ISBN 0 11 330622 9
Applying Soft Systems Methodology to an SSADM Feasibility Study	ISBN 0 11 330601 6
Automating SSADM projects	ISBN 0 11 330637 7
A Guide to SSADM and Information Systems Procurement	ISBN 0 11 330627 X
CASE and the Issues for IS Management	ISBN 0 11 330594 X
CDIF – An Overview	ISBN 0 11 330620 2
Customising SSADM	ISBN 0 11 330664 4
Database Language SQL Explained	ISBN 0 11 330583 4
Distributing Systems: Application Development	ISBN 0 11 330623 7
Estimating on SSADM Projects	ISBN 0 11 330631 8
Estimating Using Mk II Function Point Analysis	ISBN 0 11 330578 8
GEMINI: Controlling KBS Development Projects	ISBN 0 11 330591 5
GEMINI: Managing KBS Development Projects	ISBN 0 11 330592 3
GEMINI: Technical Reference	ISBN 0 11 330593 1
GEMINI in an SSADM Environment	ISBN 0 11 330638 5
Guide to SSADM Version 4 Tools Conformance Scheme	ISBN 0 11 330589 3
Improving the Maintainability of Software	ISBN 0 11 330585 0
Management of Software Maintenance	ISBN 0 11 330584 2
Managing Reuse	ISBN 0 11 330616 4
Migrating from SSADM Version 3 to Version 4	ISBN 0 11 330576 1
PCTE – An Overview	ISBN 0 11 330595 8
Prototyping Within an SSADM Environment	ISBN 0 11 330582 6
Quality Management for PRINCE and SSADM Projects	ISBN 0 11 330580 X
Reuse in SSADM Using Object-Orientation	ISBN 0 11 330621 0
Reverse Engineering – An Overview	ISBN 0 11 330602 4
SSADM and Application Packages	ISBN 0 11 330626 1
SSADM and Capacity Planning	ISBN 0 11 330577 X

SSADM and Client/Server Applications	ISBN 0 11 330624 5
SSADM and GUI Design: A Project Manager's Guide	ISBN 0 11 330650 4
SSADM for Handling Geographic Information	ISBN 0 11 330613 X
SSADM in an IS Strategy Environment	ISBN 0 11 330579 6
SSADM Version 4 Roles	ISBN 0 11 330581 8
Testing Criteria for the SSADM Version 4	ISBN 0 11 330590 7
Using CRAMM with SSADM	ISBN 0 11 330629 6
Using SSADM with PRINCE	ISBN 0 11 330598 2

NCC Blackwell Ltd., 108 Cowley Road, Oxford OX4 1JF

3GL Program Design in an SSADM Environment	ISBN 185554 7066
Euromethod in Practice	ISBN 185554 7074
Managing IS Development and Acquisition	ISBN 185554 7082
The RECAST Method for Reverse Engineering	ISBN 185554 7058

Index